T0030180

FUM D'ESTAMPA PRESS

POETRY & PROSE

'I'll say it straight off: it's one of the best poems that I have read in a long time, a long walk.'
Josep Maria Fonalleras, El Periódico

'The poem, wisely constructed, is full of symbolic images working their magic like a *memento mori*.'
Miquel Àngel Llauger, Diari Ara

'Llavina's best book, in both prose and verse.'
Manuel Cuyàs, El Punt Avui

'A densely complex spiderweb of emotions for the "sense of time", the whole poem flows towards a delta of acceptance, serenity and recognition.'
Àlex Susanna, El Mundo

'Control and chaos. Franciscanism and Darwinism. Maturity and precipitousness. Digested failures and celebrated hope. Solitude and patrimony. Truth and famine within each verse.'
Esteve Miralles, Núvol

About the Author

Jordi Llavina Murgadas (Gelida, 1968) studied Catalan Language at the University of Barcelona. He is a journalist, writer, poet, literary critic, teacher and doting father. An important and active member of the Catalan literary scene, he has been awarded a number of prizes, including the *Premi Vicent Andrés Estellés* in 2011, the *Premi de la Crítica* in 2013 and the prestigious *Lletre d'Or* in 2019 for his poem *L'Ermita* (*The Hermitage*). He lives and works in Vilafranca del Penedès.

Poetry & Prose
JORDI LLAVINA

Translation by William Hamilton

FUM D'ESTAMPA PRESS LTD.

The Hermitage was first published in Catalan
under the title *Ermita* by Editorial Meteora 2017

The Pomegranate was first published in Catalan
under the title *El magraner* by Cossetània Edicions 2020

This translation has been published in Great Britain
by Fum d'Estampa Press Limited 2020

001

Copyright © Jordi Llavina Murgadas
Translation copyright © Fum d'Estampa Press, 2019

The moral right of the author and translators has been asserted
Set in Minion Pro by Raimon Benach

Printed and bound by TJ International Ltd, Padstow, Cornwall
A CIP catalogue record for this book is available from the British Library

Fum d'Estampa Press

ISBN: 978-1-9162939-0-8

Series cover design has been inspired by the *rajola catalana*, a traditional
terracotta tile design used throughout the region.

Fum d'Estampa Press is dedicated to promoting and celebrating
Catalan culture, literature and language.

FUM D'ESTAMPA PRESS

www.fumdestampa.com

Contents

Translator's Perspective

Translating poetry is never an easy task. A good translation of any kind of text requires a deep understanding of both the source and destination language, and a flair for writing: a good poetry translation requires something more. I have been lucky to have been able to work closely with Jordi on both *The Hermitage* and *The Pomegranate Tree* and thank him for his patience and detailed explanations. Both *The Hermitage* and *The Pomegranate Tree* have offered unique challenges to me as a translator, but in a way they both share many of the same themes: death, loss, memory, nature and love, among many others. At their most basic, they are both meditations of mankind's mortality.

The Hermitage was written originally as a long poem of one sole stanza, with eight syllables per line. In Catalan, the syllables are counted only up until the last accented syllable. As such, to our English ears, the Catalan original may appear to have more than eight. In my translation, however, I have stuck rigidly to the eight-syllable rule, despite the difficulties that this has inevitably caused me. I feel, however, that it has been more than worth the extra effort due to the strength and rhythm that the poem now shows. Jordi Llavina – as all great poets so often are – is equally obsessed with language itself as he is with other, more poetic, themes. We find throughout *The Hermitage* references to certain words and phrases (particularly lines 66 to 74) that have been impossible to translate without losing the meaning of the verses in their entirety. As such, I have left these words untranslated and I urge the reader to revel in these small glimpses of the original sitting in amongst the translation.

As a poet, Jordi works closely with personal experience and this comes across in droves in *The Hermitage*. The dusty slope that he climbs up over the course of the poem is, to him, the bringer of memories – both bitter and sweet – and he expertly combines them to the surrounding environment to provide us with a uniquely in depth commentary of Catalan culture, nature and lifestyle. But more than that, his unique voice and the rhythm that the poem creates within the mind provides us with the opportunity to read a Catalan poet at the very height of his powers.

*

Compared to *The Hermitage*, *The Pomegranate Tree* is a very different beast, offering up various challenges, but of a different nature. The first to say is that Jordi's prose writing does not lend itself to easy translation as it is both complex and highly poetic. As such, when translating the story it has been important for me to remember that he is, first and foremost, a poet and that, therefore, the story should be treated as such, despite it being mostly in prose. Depicting a man on a journey around a distant but somewhat familiar Catalonia, *The Pomegranate Tree* is not an easy story to categorise.

Firstly, it has been written in both poetic stanzas and prose. The poems are used to break up the short 'chapters' but also offer the author an opportunity to bring the reader the thoughts and emotions of the main character, our Wanderer. Secondly, its use of different tenses plays with the reader to create a certain confusion regarding the passage of time throughout the story. This is something that the author has done on purpose so as to reflect the Wanderer's own admission that his journey 'was not necessarily a journey through space, but rather a journey through time.' Finally, the subject matter of the short story is very much open to debate. It is both a ghost story and a philosophical meditation on the meaning and life, love and death and where we can find ourselves when we fall through the cracks. On another level, it is also a beautiful, almost melancholic description of northern Catalonia's rugged, barren landscapes, the flora and fauna that one can come across, and the people who live there.

It is a challenging piece of writing that provides the reader – and the translator – with new insights with every read and I urge the reader to enjoy its lyrical nature and to lose oneself in a side of Catalonia and Catalan literature that is often not experienced by English speakers.

W. H.

Torno a pujar, tants anys després,
sol, a l'ermita de sant Pere.
Ni un alè d'aire, i un sol cru
de juliol que em deixarà
0005   coents el coll i les espatlles
—al vespre, em tocarà patir
el formigueig de la cremor:
la pell, que sembla que bategui
com la del cor (i hauré de planye'm
0010   d'haver enfilat tors nu el pendent).
 I tanmateix és sols així
que, a voltes, ens sentim el cos:
pels muscles encetats, desperts,
vetllant en un cos adormit
0015   (i ara no m'haig de referir
a malalties rigoroses
que fan del cos fosca pastura:
tumors i plagues, càncers, úlceres)—.
De nou, segueixo aquella senda

The Hermitage

For Marta Sagarra

Lone I climb once more, years later,
up to Sant Pere's hermitage.
The air is still, and the glare of
a raw July sun will leave my
0005 neck and shoulders burnt and tender.
At dusk, I will start to suffer
from their idle burning prickle:
my skin, throbbing to the thud of
my heartbeat. How I'll rue having
0010 scaled the slope, my torso exposed.
And yet, it's often only so
that, at times, we feel our bodies
through the crimson, attentive flesh
watching over our sleeping souls.
0015 (By this I make no reference
to the violent afflictions that
from mortal frame make dark pasture:
tumours, plagues, cancers and ulcers).
Again, I follow the footpath

que havia pres tantes vegades:
llavors, però, jo era molt jove,
i els garrofers, fragant capçada,   GARROFERS
d'on abastàvem el fruit fosc
per rosegar un xic de dolçor,
i els pins ferits d'escorça on dúiem
—tot imitant, inconscients,
l'incrèdul sant Tomàs— dos dits
per envescar-nos amb resina
la pell del clot de la mà esquerra
—amb l'altra, capturàvem, àvids,
algun insecte, al vol o a terra,
amb l'objectiu d'empresonar-l'hi—,
i les alzines centenàries,
que dècades de vent decanten,
i els roures alts d'aquest vessant
de la muntanya des del qual
pots albirar, a un tir de ballesta,
l'altre vessant —de la Mussara—,
feien, també, tots aquests arbres,
molts anys abans, l'ombra més jove
en l'espai blanc i extens del temps.
I he vist un esquirol que duia
una avellana encara verda
embolicada amb la caputxa
ben arrapada, i he sentit
arreu el cor de les cigales,   CIGALES
que és la salmòdia de l'estiu
i l'himne assedegat dels dies
de més sopor de la canícula

0020 I had wandered so many times:
I was then very young and I
recall carobs, fragrant headed,   CAROBS
from which we collected dark fruits,
sweet morsels on which to nibble,
0025 and the rough pine bark where we ran,
innocently imitating
doubting Saint Thomas, two fingers
with which to daub the hollow in
the plain of our palms with resin.
0030 With other fingers we ensnared
different insects, winged or no,
so as to imprison them there
in the centenary holm oaks,
bent over by decades of wind.
0035 And from these mountainous oaks, sat
high on this bluff, one can almost
make out, as straight as the crow flies,
the other slope, the Mussara.
And years ago, too, all these trees
0040 once cast their ever-young shadows
onto time's white, pervasive space.
And I've seen a squirrel bearing
a still-green, unripe hazelnut
wrapped up tight in its tarnished hood,
0045 and I have heard the constant choirs
of ubiquitous cicadas,   CICADAS
the droning of their summer psalms
and their parched daily hymn to the
drowsiest dog days of the year.

0050   (Machado —l'immortal— del cant
de les cigales, tan monòton,
va dir en un dels seus versos que era
un so "entre metal y madera").
I tot això m'ha fet pensar
0055   que som molt lluny dels animals
que viuen en la llibertat
dels boscos, dels barrancs, dels trossos;
i tot plegat m'ha fet concloure
que som ben lluny d'aquesta vida
0060   que a l'alba veus florir en els marges,
en un tou verd, i que, a la tarda,
ja haurà caigut marcida a terra.
Tan vagarós, m'he preguntat
què ho fa, que tinguin alguns arbres
0065   dos gèneres; que això canvïi
segons si un *oliver* fa arrels
al sud o creix una *olivera*
a la part nord d'aquest país.
¿Per què alguns cops n'he dit pomera
0070   i uns altres cops m'ha abellit més
dir-ne *pomer*? ¿Per quins set sous
hi ha uns arbres que no tenen més
que un gènere: *morera* i *plàtan*?
¿Per què, d'aquest darrer, se'n diu
0075   com de la fruita que no fa?
Si n'és, la llengua, d'arbitrària
—pensava jo, tot ascendint
pel dret camí que du a l'ermita—!
Quan sigui dalt, podré albirar,

CONTRADA

0050   (The timeless Machado, in verse,
once declared that the monotone
whining of the cicada fell
somewhere 'betwixt metal and wood'.)
And these thoughts have moved me to muse
0055   how far removed we are from the
creatures that live in the freedom
of the forests, the cliffs, the fields;
inspiring me, hence, to conclude
our distant exile from this life
0060   that dawns blushing green at the brink
before dropping and withering
to the ground by the afternoon.
How peculiar, I've wondered,
that some trees are so awarded
0065   two genders; switching names whether
an *oliver* has southern roots
or if an *olivera* sprouts
in the northern parts of our land.
Why, betimes, say I *pomera*
0070   when at others I employ the
name *pomer*? Why in all the world
are there those trees with only one
gender: *morera* and *plàtan*?
Why is it we name this last tree
0075   after a fruit it doesn't bear?
How arbitrary our tongue is,
I thought, ascending the narrow
track that leads to the hermitage!
When I reach the top, I will spy,

0080   en primer terme, la ciutat
        de Reus —i, encara més ençà,
        el poble d'Almoster, que em du
        records plaents de tants estius
        en què menjàvem per sopar
0085   les millors coques amb recapte
        que ha sabut fer la mà d'un home
        i que han sortit mai de cap forn—,
        i sé que, al fons, tocant a mar
        —que ara una gasa de calitja
0090   deu mig velar—, l'antiga Tàrraco
        aguanta, ferma, amb arrels fondes
        i el seu brancam de pedra clara.
        Que diferents aquells carreus
        de la pedrera alba del Mèdol
0095   —volums massissos, estructura—
        d'aquesta llicorella pobra   LLICORELLA
        que em vaig trobant en la pujada
        i que només ens serviria
        per fer el llosat d'una cabana,
0100   però no pas cap monument
        ni fonaments per a una casa!
        Però és la pedra del camí
        que mena a Sant Pere del Puig,
        i me l'estimo, laminosa,
0105   com també estimo, engrunadissos,
        alguns records petits de vida:
        ara em ve al cap que, essent molt jove,
        anys de la meva adolescència,
        devia ser un dissabte fred

0080   at first, the city of Reus and,
still closer to me, the village
of Almoster, a place that prompts
happy memories of summers
when for supper we would consume
0085   the very best salted *coques*
ever made by the hand of man,
that have ever left an oven.
And I know that, down by the sea,
now no doubt half concealed by a
0090   misty glaze, ancient Tarraco
remains firm, with its deep-set roots
and its bundles of bright white stone.
What contrast between those blocks once
cut out of the pale-white Mèdol
0095   – huge volumes, towering structures –
and this impoverished slate that   SLATE
I come across on my way up,
serving no use for anything
but for laying tiles on a hut,
0100   useless for both grand monuments
and the foundations of houses!
But it is the stone of this path
that leads to Sant Pere del Puig
and I love the layers of slabs
0105   as I love, too, crumbling away,
some of life's modest memories:
now I recall when, very young,
during my adolescent years,
indeed on one cold Saturday

0110 d'hivern, jo vaig endur-me a casa
      un tros cairat de llicorella
      collit al marge del camí.
      Després de netejar-lo bé
      sota el raig d'aigua d'una aixeta,
0115 va fer servei durant molts anys,
      damunt la taula de l'estudi,
      com a pitjapapers que em duia
      records d'un dia a la muntanya
      i que, fidel, un si és no és
0120 triangular, a mi em guardava
      —domèstica àncora— de perdre
      mai els papers: *la Pedra*, en deia,
      amb pe majúscula, senzill
      lligam amb el país d'estiu
0125 que és el de les arrels maternes
      —modesta i tot, hi ha una noblesa
      en una pedra de pissarra:
      és un hostal de les paraules,
      ànima i lloc de l'escriptura!—.
0130 (No em deia, aquell bocí de pedra,
      memento mori, sinó *memini*).
      Mentre recordo o bé rumio,
      segueixo ruta amunt, i faig
      una troballa: en la pols blanca
0135 del meu sender, i entre uns quants còdols
      —còdols que em fan pensar en un túmul—,
      jau un llagost de color verd
      que un negre exèrcit de formigues
      ha conquerit, i ara devora

0110 in winter, I took home with me
a rough-split piece of slate I had
retrieved from the side of the path.
And after scrubbing it up well
under a spurt of tap water,
0115 it served for many years, sitting
on the table in my study,
as a paperweight, reminding
me of a day in the mountains
and, ever faithfully, mostly
0120 triangular shaped, it stopped me,
that household anchor, from ever
losing it. *The Stone*, I would say
with a capital *S*, a stark
link to the landscape of summer,
0125 the land of my maternal roots.
Modest to a fault, humble slate
exudes a proud nobility:
a place of rest for weary words,
and the heart and soul of writing!
0130 (I named that rock shard *memini*,
in no way *memento mori*).
While I think back or ruminate,
I follow the path up and make
a find. In the dusty whiteness
0135 of my track, amongst the pebbles
that remind me of ancient tombs,
lies a green coloured grasshopper
that a black company of ants
has laid low and now ravages

0140 (la vida, sempre afamegada;
la mort, rotant d'estar ben farta!).
Veig que, en l'altura, ve un estol
de color d'ombra d'estornells.   ESTORNELLS
¿Quin és el pes d'aquests ocells
0145 que enfosquen l'aire amb el seu vol?
¿I el de la teva por, que sura
en l'aigua morta de la ment
o va excavant-te el pensament,
famèlica com una fura?
0150 (Cal que confessi que els vuit versos
que acabeu de llegir van néixer
lluny del camí que du a l'ermita.
També, però, van fer-se —amb rima
i tot— en un camí fressat,
0155 prop de la casa dels meus fills,
tocant a l'aigua del riu Bitlles
que ja no fa moure turbines
ni bategar el cor de cap fàbrica,
el dia de Nadal del 15.)
0160 I ara voldria deixar escrita
alguna cosa sobre l'aigua,   AIGUA
alguna cosa més que encara
no s'hagi compost mai, ni dit.
Alguna cosa, a més, que llisqui
0165 —si pogués fer una cosa gràcil
i que pesés, a la vegada
(pinacle i contrafort ensems),
plena de gràcia literària!—,
que llisqui damunt l'aigua sempre

0140 – life, always famished; death belches
in full-bellied satisfaction!
I see, on high, a shadowy
chattering of starlings in flight.   STARLINGS
What great weight have these birds that they
0145 darken the air with their soaring?
And what of your fear that prospers
in the dead water of your mind
or that eats away at your thoughts,
as famished as a poor ferret?
0150 (I should acknowledge that the eight
verses you have just read were born
far from the path that leads up to
the hermitage, but were written,
rhythm and all, on the well-worn
0155 paths not far from my children's home,
close to the gushing Bitlles stream
that no longer makes turbines turn
or the hearts of factories beat,
on Christmas Day twenty fifteen.)
0160 And so now I would like to jot
down something on water, something   WATER
that's never before been thought of,
never composed, never uttered.
Something, what's more, that slips and slides
0165 – if I but wrote something comely
but substantial at the same time,
both the pinnacle and buttress,
bursting with literary grace! –
and glides always on the water

0170 —aigua de vers, poema-riu—
  igual que un peix de colors vius
  o el reflex verd de l'espigat
  fullatge esborradís d'un àlber.
  (He dit: "voldria deixar escrita
0175 alguna cosa sobre l'aigua"
  —una manera de dir ambigua
  o delicadament equívoca:
  ¿hi ha cap poeta del meu segle
  que no hi escrigui, sobre l'aigua?—.
0180 Seria bo poder compondre
  damunt el glaç d'una nit crua
  perquè durés, allò que dic,
  fins que ho fongués el dit del sol
  a l'hora encesa del migdia!
0185 Claror del vers, cal·ligrafia.)
  Que vull deixar al paper —llegiu
  Palau i Fabre, l'alquimista!—
  tota la sang, vull confiar-la
  al dret relat que és el meu llibre,
0190 que, fins fa poc, ha dut el títol
  de Fato de la meva vida
  —un nom que feia so d'herència,
  de l'aire carregat dels anys,
  dens de perfums, emmaleït
0195 de fum de coses que han cremat,
  de la pudor de cors negats
  (bé que, al final, n'he dit Ermita:
  volia objectivar amb un símbol
  idees, fets, records, mancances;

0170 (water in verse, a river-rhyme)
like a vibrantly coloured fish
or the green tinge of the full-grown
foliage of the poplar tree.
As I said: 'I would like to write
0175 down something on water', which is
an ambiguous or slightly
erroneous way of saying:
is there a poet from my time
who has not written on water?
0180 How choice it would be to compose
verse on the ice of a raw night
that it might last, that which I write,
until the sun's fingers melt it
all away in the midday heat!
0185 Lightness of verse, calligraphy.
I wish to set down on paper –
read the great Palau i Fabre! –
all of my blood, entrust it to
the honest prose that is my book
0190 that, until only recently,
bore the name *Facets of my Life*,
a name hinting at legacy,
at the heavy weight of the years,
thick with diverse scents, deathly sick
0195 from the smoke of burnt-out objects,
from the stench of hopeless heartache.
What luck it's now called *Hermitage*.
I embody with a symbol:
notions, deeds, memories, wanting.

0200   un símbol —ho anireu veient—
que cal mirar en el contrallum
de l'esperança. I passo envant).
Serà una sang vessada i fosca   SANG
que ha començat a fermentar
0205   no en el sepulcre de cap llibre,
sinó en el cup del que llegiu
igual que el most fermenta en vi;
serà una sang amb gust de tinta,
tota llardosa d'hores mortes,
0210   evocadora de corrents
pertorbadors i de ressaques,
deutora de l'esclat dels cossos
que he conegut i que he estimat
i de la llum, i de la fosca,
0215   i del brogit, i del silenci
de la meva ànima, una fàbrica   ÀNIMA
tan llòbrega, a vegades tètrica,
i hospitalària altres vegades
com una cambra amb molta llum
0220   anònima d'algun hotel
d'una ciutat, posem per cas,
atlàntica i polida (Bergen,
port de postal), o també atlàntica
i rovellada (la Lisboa
0225   que vaig conèixer l'any noranta),
o atlàntica i majestuosa
(Bordeus, temple europeu del vi,
parada i fonda d'un meu somni);
sang de poema enquadernada

0200   A symbol, as you soon will see,
        that must be viewed against the light
        of hope. And ever I move on.
        It will be dark, cascading blood   BLOOD
        that started its fermentation
0205   not in the tomb of any book
        but in the press of what you read
        where the juice ferments into wine.
        It will be blood that tastes of ink,
        heavy with grease from the dead hours,
0210   evocative of confusing
        currents and hangovers due to
        the clashing of bodies that I
        have known and that I have cherished
        and of the light and of the dark,
0215   of the tumult and of the calm
        of my soul, a factory so   SOUL
        gloomy, at times so despondent,
        and others so hospitable
        like a well-lit, anonymous
0220   chamber in some nameless hotel
        in a city, for example,
        Atlantic and well-kept (Bergen,
        that postcard port); or Atlantic
        and rundown (the Lisbon that I
0225   discovered in nineteen ninety);
        or Atlantic and majestic
        (Bordeaux, that cathedral of wine
        and sanctuary of my dreams).
        Blood from a book bound poem from

0230 que he hagut de desenquadernar-me,
abans, del que en diríem l'ésser.
Volia dir, però, la joia,
aspiro a dir la meravella
—en aquest meu registre en vers—
0235 de l'aigua quan fa via, a lloure,
per un camí o per un carrer,
l'aigua que es menja tanta terra,
als camps, tot promovent torrents,
i que s'empassa arrels i còdols,
0240 escuts d'escorça, pinyes, molsa,
que transfigura els corriols
embardissats —la pau del bosc,
la seva quietud torbada,
sovint, pel grall d'algun ocell,
0245 per un sobtat esbatec d'ales—,
aquella mena de silenci
ric de murmuris, expectant,
ple de cruixits de branques seques,
de veus d'insectes —cant, brunzit—,
0250 de fresses d'invisibles rèptils
en esmunyir-se entre les herbes...
l'aigua que torna tot això
de sobte música de còrrecs,
i que absorbeix silenci i sons;
0255 aigua del vers de Ramon Llull   LLULL
"que ha en costuma que decórrega
a enjús" i que no veu mai l'hora
de fer-ho a l'inrevés, *a ensús*;
l'aigua que en viles costaneres

0230   which I must unbind myself and
all that which we might call being.
I wanted to assert the joy
and I've tried to show the wonder,
in this recited verse of mine,
0235   of water when it runs freely
down a path or along a street,
water that, devouring the earth
and the pastures, creates torrents
and swallows up roots and pebbles,
0240   shields of bark, pinecones, and mosses,
that transfigures the overgrown
narrow pathways. The peace in the
forest, its calm stillness, ruptured
oft by the squawking of some bird,
0245   an unexpected flap of wings,
that special kind of noiselessness,
rich with murmurs, expectations,
full of the crunch of dry branches,
of insect voices, songs, buzzing,
0250   of the noise of invisible
reptiles sliding through the grasses.
The water that transforms all this
at once into musical rills,
absorbing the sounds and silence,
0255   the water in Ramon Llull's verse   LLULL
'that has the tendency to run
downwards' and that never has time
to do the opposite, *upwards.*
The water that, in coastal towns,

0260 es mostra tan impietosa
quan fa d'una avinguda rambla
per al seu trànsit enfurit,
brunyint els llits d'asfalt i pedra,
arrossegant cotxes i branques,
0265 de tant en tant un deslligat
(un gos) o aquell senyal de trànsit
desarrelat pel puny del vent;
l'aigua que en tants pobles de mar,
com un recader irat, hi ha cops
0270 que fa baixar fins ran de platja
penyores tristes del bosc pròxim
—arrels i branques, herba, rama—,
l'aigua, també, que sil·labeja
en caure, de l'arbreda, poc
0275 després d'haver patit tempesta,
de la capçada dels avets,
de la dels pins, feta escorrim,
o la que canta, enfervorida
—Carner en diria que *gorgola*—,
0280 pels altaveus fondos de pedra
de gàrgoles de catedral
en capitals antigues, l'aigua
que sobreïx als embornals
i fa vessar les clavegueres
0285 amb una fètida marea,
que corroeix el ferro nu
en tantes de ciutats burgeses,
aigua del temps, filaberquí
constant de gotes que trepana

0260   is so impetuous that it
uses the *Rambla* avenue
for its own furious journey,
burnishing stony asphalt beds,
dragging with it cars and branches,
0265   now and then something left unleashed
(a dog?) or road sign that has been
uprooted by a gust of wind.
Water that, in countless seaside
towns, like an irate errand boy,
0270   causes to run down to the beach
the sad bonds from a nearby wood:
all roots and branches, weeds and boughs.
Water, too, that enunciates
when falling from woodland, not long
0275   since having suffered from a storm,
from the bouquets of fir branches,
and from those of the pines, dripping,
or that which sings passionately
– Carner would say that it *gargles* –
0280   from the profound stony speakers
of the cathedral gargoyles in
ancient capitals, the water
that overflows the scuppers and
inundates the gutters and drains
0285   with a rank, stinking tidal slick,
corroding the nude ironwork
in so many bourgeois cities.
Water of time, a constant stream
of drips that endlessly drill out

0290   l'ànima antiga de la pedra
       i la va fent emmalaltir,
       tanta aigua que podreix parracs
       d'abric de vagabund i l'ànim
       dels rodamons, l'aigua que fa
0295   desbordar rius i cegar els ulls
       dels ponts que ha fet cedir. Malhaja
       l'aigua que ens deixa a la intempèrie,
       la que marcà la meva vida
       en aquells dies tan convulsos
0300   de l'any, diria, dos mil quatre
       —*el foc té aturador, que l'aigua*
       (segons ens diu l'adagi) *no*—;
       i que, un cop més, em va fer entendre
       una lliçó ben valuosa:
0305   som aigua, un flux, a penes —feble—,
       d'aigua normal i corrent, aigua
       que sempre ha de fer via avall
       —potser, com deia el clàssic, som
       un somni, sí, un somni llisquent
0310   entre el no-res i el buit—, un curs
       d'aigua que corre cap enlloc,
       presa del temps, d'aquella pressa
       de l'any de l'hora del segon,
       que hem de fer tantes coses bones
0315   abans no se'ns assequi el cos
       —la pell la carn la sang— i l'ànima,
       i no hàgim tingut temps de fer-les,
       i ens acabem trobant, a l'últim,
       una riera seca, eterna

0290   the archaic soul of the stones,
making them fall into illness;
the water that rots the beggar's
tattered coat and the wanderer's
courage; the water that causes
0295   rivers to burst and blinds the eyes
of bridges long since given up.
Damn the water that bares us all,
that which so marked my life during
those convulsed, unsettled days of
0300   the year, I'd say twenty oh four
– *a fire can be stopped, but water*
(according to the adage) *can't* –
and that, once again, taught me a
very valuable lesson:
0305   we are water, hardly a weak
flow of routine water, water
that always must run off downward.
Perhaps, as is oft said, we are
but a dream, yes, a dream that slips
0310   between nothing and the void, a
flow of water, running nowhere,
running out of time, that yearly
rush of each hour and second, in
which we have to do countless tasks
0315   before our bodies shrivel up –
skin, meat and blood, body and soul –
and we've not had time to do them.
And thus, in the end, we're left with
a dried-up stream, an eternal

0320 tomba per l'aigua que vam dur
(una aigua vívida, avui morta!)
Deia que aquella temporada,
com un escura-xemeneies
que —traïdor— es vesteix de lladre,
0325 l'aigua es tornà un subtil intrús
que fa entrar la malura a casa.
Principalment pel carener
de la teulada, les goteres
van afectar diverses zones
0330 del dúplex del carrer de Sant
Bernat, al cor de Vilafranca.
Porfidiós —escorrialles
negres de pluja, degoteig—,
aquell malson d'aigua va atènyer
0335 uns quants volums que emmerletaven
dos mòduls de la llibreria
del pis de dalt del meu estudi
—la poesia portuguesa
i alguns catàlegs de pintura:
0340 Eugénio de Andrade i Rothko   ROTHKO
tenen, per mi, poemes, quadros
i uns blancs de pàgina ensutzats
per tot de taques d'aigües àcides—,
i em va bufar el parquet del terra.

0345 I ara, en la meva ascensió
pel dret camí que du a l'ermita
de Sant Pere del Puig —encara
no se'n pot veure la carcassa
(de mas més que no pas de temple)

0320 tomb for the water we once bore
 – a water once alive, now dead.
 I was referring to that time
 when, just as a chimney sweep who,
 snake-like, donned a thief's garb, water
0325 became a subtle intruder
 that brought sickness into my home.
 In the main, through the peak or ridge
 of the roof, the water droplets
 affected a number of parts
0330 of the duplex on Carrer de
 Sant Bernat in the very heart
 of Vilafranca. Obstinate
 dregs of black rain, constant dripping,
 that watery nightmare ravaged
0335 a number of volumes that crowned
 two parts of the bookcase that stood
 on the floor above my study –
 my Portuguese poetry and
 some catalogues about painting.
0340 My Rothko and Eugénio   ROTHKO
 de Andrade books now have lines,
 drawings and some blank leaves daubed by
 the stain of acidic water –
 and it wrinkled the parquet floor.

0345 And I continue, now, to climb
 up the straight pathway that leads to
 Sant Pere's hermitage. I am
 still yet to see its outer shell
 – more of a *Mas* than a temple –

0350 rere els xiprers empolsegats
que fan, tan rigorosos, guàrdia
davant la llar de Déu—, aquí
i allà el meu peu va ensopegant
amb tot d'arrels de pins molt vells   ARRELS
0355 que el temps, més vell encara —antic—,
s'ha escarrassat a descolgar.
Sota el crostim de terra i pedra
del meu camí, dessota un tel
de pols que dura tot l'estiu,
0360 formen relleus que em fan pensar
en unes venes excitades
de virior, venes de mans
i braços de ferrer —tibants
com una corda en una vela—
0365 que, de tan tenses, sempre tems
si no els han d'esqueixar la pell,
venes dels homes que treballen
picant ferro roent, el ferro
que es blega dòcilment i es corba
0370 en una encesa ferradura,
homes que em fan considerar
l'arrel del seu braó, atàvica,
semblants als que pintà Velázquez   VELÁZQUEZ
en una tela al·lucinada
0375 (la forja crua del dolor
i el mall que encerta el moll de l'ésser).
¿On és que van, lluny de les soques,
de la fondària de la terra,
totes aquestes rels que fugen,

0350   behind the dusty cypress trees
that so rigorously stand guard
before that house of God. Here and
there my foot bumps into and rubs
up all the elderly pine roots   ROOTS
0355   that time, earlier still, ancient,
has worked tirelessly to unpick.
And 'neath the crust of earth and stone
on my path, under a fabric
of dust that lasts through summer long,
0360   reliefs develop that remind
me of vigorous, excited
veins, capillaries from the hands
or arms of a working blacksmith,
rigid like rigging under sail,
0365   that, under such strain, one always
worries might lacerate the skin,
the veins of men who labour at
pounding red-hot iron, iron
that bends and curves submissively
0370   into burning, red-hot horseshoes,
men who force me to muse on the
roots of their arms, atavistic,
as if painted by Velázquez   VELÁZQUEZ
on a dream-like canvas mirage.
0375   The crude forge of anguish and the
club that beats the crux of the soul.
Where do they go, far from the trunk,
from the very depths of the earth,
all of these roots that run away,

0380 arrels que repten, serps de llenya
immòbils, ertes? Es diria
que s'han ben atipat de fosca
i han decidit posar-se dretes.
Trenta anys enrere, hi vaig trobar
0385 —arrels indòmites, rebels,
que malden per conèixer com
deu ser la vida d'una branca—
un agafall per al meu ànim,
el passamà per no estimbar-me
0390 en tants d'abismes de la pensa,
empelt del cor al fonament
de l'arbre i, més encara, exemple
(el més preuat dels d'aquella època):
llavors, de noi, el meu designi
0395 solia ser desaferrar-me,   DESAFERRAR-SE
desaferrar-me de la terra,
desaferrar-me dels diners
que no em servien per comprar
el que aspirava a posseir,
0400 desaferrar-me d'uns veïns
portadors d'ànimes de xai,
tot fent escarafalls i ganyes
de llop esquàlid i impotent;
desaferrar-me, sobretot,
0405 del temps (l'amic Jordi Llobet
fa poc va confessar-me —admeto
que jo no en recordava res—
d'haver-me vist secretament
plorar davant una foguera

0380 these crawling roots, these immobile,
rigid, firewood snakes? It might be
that they've taken their fill of the
dark and decided to rise up.
Thirty years ago, I found there
0385 – indomitable rebel roots,
determined to discover what
the life of a branch might be like –
a hardy grip on my spirit,
a handrail so as not to fall
0390 into so many voids of thought,
a spliced heart at the foot of the
trees and, what's more, an example
(the most valued one from that time),
of the boy I once was. Back then
0395 I wished to separate myself,   SEPARATE
take myself away from the Earth,
remove myself from the money
that I could not use to purchase
that which I aspired to possess,
0400 remove myself from the neighbours
whose tiresome sheep-like spirits once
exaggerated and fussed and
gurned like squalid, impotent wolves.
Separate myself, most of all,
0405 from time. My friend Jordi Llobet
recently told me – I admit
that I recalled nothing at all –
that he had seen me secretly
cry, standing before a bonfire

0410 en una nit d'estiu (potser
de l'any vuitanta-tres) al bell
mig de la plaça del Pedró
—el punt més alt de l'escenari
romànticament envoltat
0415 de les ruïnes del castell
del poble de Gelida—. Rostre
amagadís, vaig contestar-li
que la raó del meu plor esquiu
era haver entès que el temps ens crema
0420 a foc dramàticament lent.   FOC
Adolescent presumptuós,
plorava —incògnit— per ser vist:
un fil lligava —imperceptible
als ulls dels altres nois— la flama
0425 alada i la terrenca brasa
amb el meu plany, l'íntima crema
de la foguera compartida
—que enlluernava la rotllana
de cares tristes que cantaven
0430 i alegres cossos que sentien
fondes punyides de desig:
el foc il·luminava l'ésser—   ÉSSER
amb el secret que començava
a encendre's en la meva ment,
0435 en el meu pensament, pels anys
que feien via, en el meu cor
pel sentiment del temps que, en suma,   TEMPS
devia començar a patir
de nen —assumpte del meu llibre).

0410 one summer night, perhaps in the
year nineteen eighty-three, slap bang
in the heart of the Pedró square,
the highest section of the stage
romantically enveloped
0415 by the ruins of the castle
in the town of Gelida. Face
hidden, I replied to him that
the reason for my timid tears
was that I'd realised that time
0420 burnt us all on a long, slow fire.   FIRE
Presumptuous adolescent,
I cried in disguise to be seen.
A wire, imperceptible to
the eyes of the other boys, joined
0425 the dancing flame and coarse embers
to my lament, the intimate
smouldering of the bonfire that
so lit up and dazzled the throng
of singing sad faces and the
0430 happy bodies feeling profound
pangs of desire, shared with the fire
illuminating our being,   BEING
the dark secret that was starting
to glow and ignite in my mind,
0435 in my mind's eye, the years leading
up to my heart enduring the
sentiment of time that, in short,   TIME
I used to suffer from as a
young child: the subject of my book.

0440 D'ençà d'aquella edat, em sé
poma de cove que té un cop.
¿Què se'n pot treure? ¿Es pot desfer
per fer-ne suc, un dolç xarop,
havent llençat, primer, la taca
0445 —d'un color fosc i rovellós—,
al pot dels fems, i així esperar que
aquell bocí de mal sangós
l'oblit el sàpiga dissoldre
per fer-ne de no-res polsim,
0450 igual que sap la pedra moldre
o el núvol arrosar amb plugim?
Tinc, doncs, un cop, com una fruita
—senyal que, lluny de condemnar-me,
em va predisposar a la lluita
0455 des que era un noi i pur, nu d'arma.

I ara, no sé per què, em ve al cap
un episodi de família
que té com a protagonista
el meu fill gran: sent un nadó,   FILL
0460 passant les hores de dormida,
solia, inconscient, tirar,
dins el bressol, el cos amunt,
reptant —morós— pel matalàs
curtíssim que l'encoixinava
0465 —vida allà dins colgada, vida
brevíssima, en dorment, del fill—,
i no parava fins que el cap
—recercador com el musell

0440 And since that age I have felt like
a bruised apple in a basket.
What can be gained from it? Can it
be pressed for juice, a sweet syrup,
having first thrown away the dark,
0445 rusty red-coloured painful stain
onto the manure pile, waiting
for oblivion to dissolve
that bloody morsel, breaking it
down to a fragment of nothing,
0450 like a grinding millstone or the
decline of a rain-sprinkled cloud?
I have, therefore, a fruit-like bruise,
a mark that, whilst not damning me,
leaves me predisposed to struggle
0455 since my childhood, pure and unarmed.

And now a family event
carelessly springs to mind in which
my eldest child plays the main rôle.
He was still a new-born baby,   SON
0460 whiling away his hours of sleep,
habitually twisting his
body upwards in his cradle,
creeping sluggishly across the
tiny mattress that held him tight.
0465 A still hidden being, my son's
momentary, brief, torpid life,
he continued until his head,
probing feverishly like a

febril d'un talp— no s'encertia
0470 d'haver-ne aconseguit tocar
el límit bla, enconxat de roba.
Un cop sentia, m'imagino,
en el seu crani d'ossos tendres
—i encara no encaixats del tot—
0475 aquell confí del primer llit
—límit inaugural, tan pròxim,
confirmat, doncs—, llavors el son
ja era tranquil tota la nit
i res podia desvetllar-lo.
0480 Voldria, doncs, deixar en els versos   LLENGUATGE
alguna mena de certesa:
pressentir el límit del llenguatge,
poder-me afigurar el topall
del que es pot dir, abans del no-res.
0485 D'aquest durable aprenentatge,
en guanyo un símbol: el detall
del fill que dorm, encara il·lès,
nen condemnat, cor pur, ostatge
del temps. La mort branda el sonall: MORT
0490 vetlla el nadó —al bressol estès—,
el té a la falda. Hòrrida imatge:
la dida droga el seu vassall.
(Compra a baix preu ombres a pes,
la mercadera del carnatge.)
0495 Jo sempre he escrit per curar el tall
que ens fa saber que no som res.

I vaig pujant, a poc a poc,
pel blanc camí que du a una ermita

mole's snout, achieved its objective
0470   of managing to reach and touch
the smooth, cloth-lined edge of the cot.
At times, I imagine he felt,
within his soft-boned cranium,
not yet all rightly set in place,
0475   those boundaries of his first bed
– inaugural limits, so close,
already confirmed – and then he
would sleep soundly throughout the night
and nothing could stir or wake him.
0480   I'd like, therefore, to set in verse   LANGUAGE
something of a certain truth. To
presage the limit of language,
to make out the mark of what can
be said before the darkness falls.
0485   From this durable instruction,
I earn a stark symbol: that of
the sleeping child, yet still unharmed,
doomed, pure of heart, a hostage to
time. Death brandishes the rattle,   DEATH
0490   cares for the child laid in the cot,
bounces it on its lap. A dark
image: the wet nurse drugs her lord.
She buys low-cost shadows by weight,
a morbid merchant of carnage.
0495   I have always written to heal
the wound that shows us to be naught.

And still I slowly upwards climb
along the white path that leads to

(és blanc de pols, i blanc de llum,
0500 llevat d'aquells moments que l'ombra
que faig en caminar hi escampa
pintura negra esborradissa,
i és que la marxa no permet
que pugui arribar-s'hi a agafar
0505 —tampoc no dura gaire mai
l'ombra del cos, de cosa viva,
damunt la terra. És un país
de dol, el món: per això, l'aigua
dels rius en fuig, esperitada—).
0510 I veig que, en un estimball, penja,
ben solitària, la flor arbrada
d'una atzavara. Em du el record   ATZAVARA
de la mangala deposada
de l'avi el dia que va caure,
0515 la nit que es va morir —bastó
de pelegrí sobre l'abisme—:
ja era una arrel lluny de la terra,
silent pesava entre jaquetes
de primavera, al penja-robes
0520 —la roba, amb gest dels vius als plecs,
i encara alguna peça seva,
hieràtica, aplomada, muda—.
Fa quaranta anys, aquesta planta
que ara ha florit, perquè ja és morta,
0525 no era tan sols ni una llavor
(llavor de mort, qualsevol planta
la porta dins, i el cor de l'ésser).
¿Per què va créixer sola, aquesta,

the hermitage. White dust, white light,
0500 lifted in those moments when my
drifting shadow casts its fleeting
black dye across the landscape, yet
its movement cannot allow it
to reach out and grasp it tightly.
0505 Not that the corporeal shade,
that living thing, ever lasts too
long upon this earth. It's a land
of grief, this world. So the waters
of the rivers do flee, possessed.
0510 And I see hanging from a cliff
the lonely wooden flower of
the agave tree. It reminds me   AGAVE TREE
of my grandfather's abandoned
walking stick on the day he fell,
0515 the night that he died, a pilgrim's
staff at the edge of the abyss.
Already a root far from earth,
it weighed silently amongst spring
jackets, there on the wardrobe hooks.
0520 The clothes, creased by the yet living,
and still some of his own pieces,
solemn, cumbersome, now silent.
Forty years ago, this plant, now
blooming in decay, in its death,
0525 was not even a lowly seed
– the seed of death carried within
all plants, at the heart of all souls.
Why did this one grow alone with

sense companya al seu redol?
0530 ¿Per què floreix i es fa més bella,
una atzavara quan es mor?
Ara el camí es torna planer,
voreja un camp d'avellaners:
soc una mica més a prop
0535 de coronar el pla de l'ermita.
Als anys de la meva noiesa,
allò era un verd esbarzerar.
Les fosques deixalles del bosc
havien pres algunes pedres
0540 desenfilades de la fàbrica
de l'enlairada esglesiola.
Com una pell de serp —despulla
abandonada—, escampats, veies
llavors, per terra, tot de trossos
0545 bruts de calçobre, unes engrunes
de la façana profanada;
anava, alhora, creixent l'herba
de les bardisses nebuloses,
alta i selvàtica, deixebla
0550 de la malesa aspra del temps.
I avui, ¿com deurà ser l'espai
que crèiem, en els nostres jocs
de nen, en memorables tardes
d'estiu, d'una altitud alpina,
0555 senyorejat per un castell
que delejàvem conquerir
—construcció de fantasia
que, essent ja gran, he retrobat

nothing to keep it company?
0530 Why does the agave flower bloom,
only showing its charm in death?
The path now starts to level out,
running by a field of almond
trees and I'm slightly closer to
0535 crowning the hermitage's plain.
Throughout all my years of boyhood
there was a green patch of brambles.
The dark remains of the forest
have carried away some stones that
0540 were loosened by the factory
which raised up the tiny chapel.
Like a snake's skin, abandoned and
nude, sprawled all over, I saw, then,
on the ground, a multitude of
0545 sullied plaster parts, crumbling chunks
of desecrated palisades.
Meanwhile, the grass was flourishing
in the dark, nebulous hedgerows,
high and sylvan, disciples to
0550 the malevolent coarseness of
time. And now, where are the places
we believed in, in our childhood
games, played over memorable
summer afternoons, alpine high,
0555 and dominated by strongholds
that we once ached to overthrow?
Fantastical constructions that,
now older, I've rediscovered

en tants castells, al país d'Oc,
0560   amb una idèntica prestància,
car tot allò que abraça l'ull
d'un nen —erm o ruïna— es torna
ferma carena de merlets
i intactes torres entrevistes
0565   des de darrere de la fusta
i el fullam d'horts de bells fruiters
en flor, mirífics, esclatants!—.
I, ara que esmento els horts, voldria   HORT
apuntar encara que el poeta
0570   —igual que un nen— és qui en té cura.
Tal com ho veig, però, el seu hort
creix en l'altura, i pren la llum
de més a prop (acull, també,
més jove, l'aigua; i la neu, pura).
0575   Aquest hort fa, per una banda,
frontera amb un penya-segat.
Solen les branques —carregades,
segons l'estació, de nespres
de pell que sembla cuir, de préssecs,
0580   de pomes verdes, de taronges,
de prunes lila o d'albercocs—
penjar, abocant-se a l'oceà   OCEÀ
(i cau madura de la branca
la dolçor closa, suïcida,
0585   de cada fruit; va rodolant,
fins que, afamada, la borrassa
de l'aigua la devora a l'acte).
A l'altra banda del seu hort,

in countless castles in the land
0560 of Occitania, matching
aspects, as all that catches a
child's eye, waste or ruin, becomes
a hardy crown of battlements
and well-built towers spied briefly
0565 from behind the thickets and the
foliage of the orchard trees
in bloom, exquisite and brimming!
And, mentioning orchards, I'd like   ORCHARD
to remark that it is, in fact,
0570 each poet, childlike, who cares for
his own. As I see it, though, each
orchard grows on high, trapping light
found close to hand (it receives, too,
more fledgling water, purer snow).
0575 These orchards, on one side, form a
boundary with a row of cliffs.
Often the branches, charged with fruit
according to the season, with
medlars and their leather-like skin,
0580 peaches, green apples, oranges,
purple plums or with apricots,
hang, running into the ocean   OCEAN
– and the enclosed sweetness of each
fruit falls, suicidal, mature,
0585 from the branch. It tumbles away
until, starving, the watery
blanket finally devours it.
The other side of this orchard

s'estén, vastíssim, un desert.   DESERT
0590 S'hi arriba per un corriol
encaixonat entre parets
altes de sal que mirallegen.
En el silenci del desert,
es pot sentir, a l'altre costat
0595 de la muntanya, més enllà
de l'hort, braolar —fonda— l'aigua.
(Ara he volgut deixar un registre
de l'hort encimbellat d'un somni
freqüent de la meva noiesa:
0600 no el regava cap riu, sinó
només l'aigua constant de pluja.
Un espadat a banda i banda.
Aquí, oceà; i allà, un desert.
D'ençà de la primera nit
0605 que vaig tenir aquell somni, he vist
que els horts que fan els homes són
còpies borroses d'aquest hort
que deixo, en usdefruit, al líric.)

I vaig fent via, camí amunt.
0610 Veig l'olivera abandonada   OLIVERA
que cap pagès no ha cuidat mai,
perquè és com l'arbre comunal
—captaire de rosada i aigua,
de pedregades, fosca i llum,
0615 de cels llampants viats de blanc
i gris de núvol— apostat
al seu revolt, que ja aleshores
malaltejava d'eixorquia,

runs away vast into desert.

0590 One reaches it by a pathway,
boxed in amongst high, salty walls
that effervesce down from on high.
In the silence of the desert,
one can hear on the other side
0595 of the mountain, still further than
the orchard, the deep roaring of
water. Now shall I leave you with
an image of the towering
grove that frequented many a
0600 childhood dream. It was fed not by
any stream, but only constant
rain. Precipices on both sides.
Here, the ocean. And there, desert.
As of the very first night that
0605 I had this dream, I have seen that
the gardens made by men are but
blurred copies of this grove that I
now leave, usufruct, on this page.

And still I follow the path up.
0610 I see the forsaken olive

tree that no farmer thinks to tend,
treated as common ground by all.
A beggar for dew and water,
for hailstorms, darkness and light, for
0615 stormy skies lit white by lightning
and grey by clouds. Dedicated
to its disturbance, already
diseased by infertility,

retort de tronc, balmat de soca,
0620 profundament balmat de soca,
on somiàvem d'amagar-hi
tresors de menudall (xavalla,
bales de vidre o fang, ceràmica
feta bocins) embolicats
0625 amb mocadors nuats (t'havia
ben oblidat, borda olivera!),
ombra serena de la ruta
que tanta soledat, de sempre,
ha embastardit —i, tot i això,
0630 conills, perdius i sargantanes
segur que deuen dedicar-li
alguns minuts de companyia
al cap de l'any; i la claror
de les estrelles i la lluna,
0635 hores senceres, fredes, càlides
(bé que potser un arbre desitja
tenir ben a tocar un company
de la seva natura: arrels
fondes en terra i rama en l'aire,
0640 baldament sigui un cep cremat,
mig escapat de la filera)—.
De nen, totes les coses semblen   NEN
—no semblen, són— més grosses i altes,
i també semblen —més ben dit,
0645 són— molt més llargues les distàncies.
Potser ens semblava una caseta
abandonada de peó,
el memorable oliver bord!

its twisted trunk, its empty stem,
0620   its deeply desolate torso
in which we once dreamed of hiding
tiny shards of treasures – loose change,
marbles of glass or mud, morsels
of pottery – all wrapped up in
0625   knotted handkerchiefs (how you had
forgotten, you grumpy old tree!).
Some serene shade on a route that
so much solitude, for so long,
has finally debased. Yet in
0630   spite of this, rabbits, partridges
and lizards no doubt dedicate
some moments to its company
throughout the year; and the brightness
coming from the moon and the stars,
0635   hours and timeless hours, sultry and
crisp. Perhaps a tree desires to
have in its grasp a companion
of its own nature: roots running
deep in the earth and branches in
0640   the air, even a charred grapevine,
worming its way out of its wire.
As a young child, everything seems   CHILD
– not seems, is – larger and higher,
and distances also seem – or,
0645   rather, are – very much greater.
And perhaps to us it seemed like
an abandoned peasant's dwelling,
that memorable, barren tree!

Tan espectral, llavors, espluga
0650   on els moixons feien estada.
Quan arribàvem en aquest
recolze del camí, ja vèiem,
encara lluny, els greus xiprers,
i reposàvem una estona
0655   estintolant-nos en la soca
de l'arbre vell, i amb una mà
encarcarada de paüra
buscàvem dins la panxa buida
de l'olivera, fins a perdre'n
0660   la visió, i llavors el tacte
se'ns feia un ull sensible a aquell
misteri franc de la natura:
escorça eixuta, escorça morta
del tronc mig escorxat... i, tan-
0665   mateix, hi havia fulles dalt,
ornant d'un verd polsós les branques.
Fèiem anar la mà per dins: POR
mai no hi vam viure la sorpresa
de tocar el cuiro d'una bossa
0670   prenyada de monedes d'or,
lligada amb un cordó vermell;
i, per fortuna, mai tampoc
no va passar que, a les palpentes,
s'esfereís la mà amb la ingrata
0675   certesa d'haver descobert
una despulla d'animal
—carn morta, ossos i pell de gat
o de guineu—, que, ben mirat,

Back then, how very spectral, that
0650 grotto where tiny birds sojourned.
When reaching this doughty crossroads
in the path we would spy the stern
cypress trees in the far distance
and we would halt for a moment,
0655 resting our bodies on the old
tree's torso and with a hand, then,
set taut and rigid in terror
we would feel blindly in the old
tree's empty paunch until losing
0660 sight of it, and from then on touch
would be our eyes astute in that
brazen mystery of nature.
A scrawny bark, bereft of life,
from a half-flayed trunk and, all the
0665 while, still leaves flourished up above,
adorning the stalks with green dust.
We slowly placed our hands inside: FEAR
never did we live to sense the
touch and feel of a leather pouch,
0670 full to the brim with golden coins
and sealed with a twist of red string.
Nor were we, luckily, groping
blindly in the dark, ever shocked
by the brush of a hand against
0675 the luckless certainty of one
having chanced upon some beast's corpse
– a cat's or a fox's dead flesh, skin
and bones – that, when closely laid bare,

era el que de debò cercàvem
0680 amb el rampell del nen que tempta
el gaudi estrany de tenir por.

He arribat, doncs, a l'olivera
de mig camí, i veig que en el cel
cremat de llum d'aquest matí
0685 d'estiu, rere una branca, hi ha,
com pàl·lid torterol de fum
que entela un vidre, gairebé
plena, una lluna que em fa entendre   LLUNA
totes les llunes dels meus anys:
0690 "Fixa-t'hi bé: rodona esbossa
—perfet— el dibuix d'una cara:
relleu dels pòmuls i del nas,
clap de blancor a la pell i el to
més fosc de les concavitats"
0695 —reprodueixo les paraules
amb què ho va dir una professora,
o mestra, de literatura
en un curs de batxillerat—.
Rostre que ens sotja nit i dia,
0700 de tant en tant encara solc
mirar-me el cel, buscant-la a ella
(costa trobar-la amb llum de dia
—sabreu tot d'una per què ho dic—,
i així acostumo a conformar-me
0705 a saludar-la en la blavor
del cel foscant, admirador
com soc de l'alta forma blanca

was that which, in truth, we sought in
0680   the child's desire to tempt and seek
out that exotic dash of fear.

And so, I've reached the olive tree
that stands halfway, and I see that
in the sky, burnt by the light of
0685   this summer morn', behind a branch
there sits, like a pallid spiral
of steam, fogging up a pane of
glass, nigh full, a moon that tells of   MOON
all of the moons of all my years.
0690   'Look closely: a circular sketch,
a perfect drawing of a face,
the outlines of cheekbones and nose,
a splash of white skin alongside
the darker tones of its caverns'.
0695   I quote words once spoken by a
baccalaureate professor
or lecturer in literature.
An observing face night and day,
from time to time I still tend to
0700   gaze up at the sky, searching for
her there – not easy is it to
find her against the light of day
(I should not need to tell you why)
and so I tend to cheer myself
0705   with a wave into the deep blue
of the sombre sky, admirer
as I am of the lofty white

que creix o minva: hi ha vegades
que sembla una aquarel·la, i d'altres
0710   se m'afigura un oli antic;
si és nova, és com la marca a l'aigua
impresa en un paper de preu),
i a fe que hi és, com aleshores;
avui, però, ja no hi veig mai
0715   —en fer ella el ple, quasi solar—
la cara de la molinera
de la cançó —una llum d'esglai
de l'enamorament— que, anys ha,
sempre sabia endevinar-hi
0720   —jove i etern, feliç, taujà—,
sinó l'expressió glaçada
i fonda d'una calavera
de nen o de ratapinyada,
desemparada en un terrari,
0725   closca d'os nua i escurada.
Vull referir-me encara a una altra
anècdota que té la lluna
com a veríssim punt de fuga
(torno a l'incís de més amunt).
0730   La meva filla, essent petita,   FILLA
acostumava a detectar-la,
al pic del dia, en la desèrtica
nuesa de la plana cèlica,
en la vastíssima buidor
0735   del pèlag de la llum immòbil.
I, de vegades, fins anant
amb cotxe sabia trobar-la:

form, waxing and waning: there are
times it seems a watercolour,
0710 and yet others an ancient oil.
As new, it's like a watermark
found pressed into costly paper –
trusting, like before, that she's there.
These days, though, I never now see,
0715 when she's full, almost solaresque,
that mill-like appearance from that
song, a light of astonishing
love and fondness that, years ago,
I always knew how to guess at
0720 – young and abiding, blessed, simple –
sooner than the frozen grimace
and backdrop of a juvenile
infant or abandoned bat skull,
left shunned in a terrarium,
0725 naked bones of scoured cranium.
I'd like, once again, to refer
to an anecdote that truly
uses the moon as a keystone.
I refer to my words above.
0730 My daughter, as a little girl,   DAUGHTER
used to seek for and locate it
at high noon, in the desert-like
bareness of the celestial
plane, in the endless emptiness
0735 of that pond of unmoving light.
And, at times, even from her seat
in the car could she pinpoint it:

en deia el lloc precís, enllà
dels arbres d'algun parc o bosc,
0740 com si el satèl·lit li imantés
la ment i el cor, a més de l'ull.
Avui trobo a faltar la filla,
l'enyoro tot buscant la forma
sagrada del lacre en l'altura
0745 que m'ha de confirmar que el cel
que llegiré com una carta
és el mateix que ha de llegir
la noia a l'hora del capvespre
en un país tan lluny del nostre.

0750 Ara el camí enfila un pendent,
i, a mà esquerra, em queda la vista
de petits masos i barraques
disseminats, com cards brostats
en el vessant solell del puig.
0755 En dies d'hivernal cruesa,
d'alguna xemeneia en surt
un fil de fum, alè de vida.
I, quan el cel d'aquest país   NEU
té ganes de nevar una mica
0760 —passa al febrer, de tard en tard—,
muden de pell teulats i ràfecs,
que se'ls fa blanca i torna crosta
(ben diferent de les teulades
del poble, on no dura la neu,
0765 i sol mudar al color de l'aigua
el blanc abans de fer-se pedra).
Penso en la neu al juliol

she would call out the exact spot,
there from beyond park or forest
0740 trees, as if the satellite was
drawn to her heart, her mind, her eyes.
Today I long for my daughter,
I miss her while I search for that
sacred waxy outline on high
0745 that confirms to me that the sky
I read as I read a letter
is the one and the same the girl
reads as dusk comes in and evening
falls in a country far from ours.

0750 The path now courses up a rise
and on my left-hand side I spy
meagre villas and scattered shacks
wedged like leafy thistles on the
sunny slopes of the mountain top.
0755 On days of wintery harshness,
from some chimney there rises up
a thread of smoke, a breath of life.
And when the heavens of this land   SNOW
assume the need to snow somewhat
0760 around late February time,
roofs and eaves themselves are re-skinned,
whitened and full crusted over
– quite different from the gables
in the village, where snow lasts not,
0765 ofttimes turning white like water
before transforming into stone.
I think of the July snow as

—com al bo de gener pensava
en l'aigua verda de les basses
0770 on vaig aprendre a capbussar-me,
i en els sopars a l'aire lliure—.
No sé si venen gaire al cas
aquests records —*par que somiï
tot quant vei pres ma faç*—. No sé
0775 si ara mateix ve gaire a tomb
el meu desvari de memòria
i pensaments: en la primera
sempre he trobat la complaença
del vi que no se'ns fa mai ranci.
0780 L'home recorda igual que pensa,   MEMÒRIA
i aquella fa que mai no es cansi
de l'amarguesa de la pensa.
El que era abans fa que ara avanci
i fins que obtingui recompensa
0785 del temps gastat i el goig que és lluny.
Quanta raó que tens, memòria!
Llei d'edat morta, avui no ens puny
allò que ahir ens feria al pit.
Les pors d'antany són pols o escòria,
0790 que una mà folla ja no ens muny
àcidament el cor de nit.
Visquem, serens, la nostra història:
que, en l'or del cor, quedi l'encuny
de la noblesa d'esperit.

0795 (Tot d'un plegat, una perdiu   PERDIU
aixeca el vol, i no s'atura:
fa cap al cel, que és com un niu

at the height of January
I pondered the green waters of
0770   the lagoons where I learnt to dive
and the fresh al fresco suppers.
I know not if these memories
are relevant – *par que somiï*
tot quant vei pres ma faç. I know
0775   not if right now this tangent of
mine, memories and reflections,
is by design: I've always come
upon, from the first, the pleasure
of wine that never turns rancid.
0780   Man recollects as he reflects,   MEMORY
suggesting that the bitterness
of his thought is ever watchful.
What was once past is now advanced
until a reward is obtained
0785   from time spent and distant pleasure.
Oh, how right you are, memory!
Law of deathly age, today hurts
us not which yesterday beat our
brows. The fears of days gone by are
0790   but dust or dirt, that a rabid
hand at night might not milk us dry.
Serenely, we live our own tales:
in the heart's eye lies the mark of
the nobility of spirit.

0795   All of a sudden, a partridge   PARTRIDGE
unceasingly takes to the air.
It soars to the heavens, a nest

per a ella i els d'igual natura.
Niu infinit, però incomplet,
0800 car no hi podria fer la posta.
S'allunya, ara, del meu indret,
ben poc després gira i s'acosta.
Estima l'aire i el terròs.
Si ara tingués una escopeta,
0805 podria despenjar-li el cos.
Per sort, duc llapis i llibreta.
Amb l'ànima ja faig, que aterra
en el meu vers mentre ella vola.
Jo també em sé una ànima que erra
0810 —si petja o vol—, i que va sola.)

I vaig seguint la meva ruta,
fent via amunt, i enlloc no sents
aigua de fonts o rierol
(la de les basses s'està al pla:
0815 des d'aquí dalt en veig brillar
l'argent, i penso en tolls —al poble
en diuen xolls— després d'un ram
d'aquells que fan, a la tardor,
més fosca l'escorça dels arbres
0820 i fangosa la terra; l'aigua
de tantes basses —adormida—
que fa engreixar les avellanes).
Només hi ha pols, al meu camí   POLS
—la pols tan blanca on va gravant-se
0825 una sanefa amb la trencada
sola d'avarca dels meus passos—,
blancor de pols i un xic de verd

for her and her natural kind.
Infinite nest, yet incomplete,
0800 unable, there, to lay her eggs.
She flies away, now, from my place
but soon after shifts and returns.
She loves the air and the terrain.
If now I had here a rifle,
0805 I could easily bring her down.
Happily, I bear but pen and
notebook. By the spirit I land
the bird in my verse while she flies.
I, too, know a wandering soul,
0810 on wing or foot, always alone.

And still I follow my pathway,
climbing up, and nowhere can one
attend water in springs or streams.
That of the pools is down on the
0815 flat and from here on high I see
shining silver, and I think of
puddles, called *xolls* in the village,
and after of those autumn wreaths
that make tree bark murkier and
0820 the earth more sodden. The water
of so many sleeping basins
from which the hazelnuts grow fat.
There is nothing but dust on my   DUST
path, white dust marked by the outline
0825 of the broken soles of my shoes,
of the *avarques* of each step,
white powder with a touch of some

de rama en l'aire, pins i alzines,
i el negre que griseja, als marges,
0830 d'aqueixa pedra llicorella
que es va desfent a cops de temps.
Si féssim —morts— la pols tan blanca
com la d'aquest camí que petjo;
i si cada un dels nostres ossos
0835 fos fet, posem per cas, de pòrfir!
Cremat, el cos fa una pols grisa
com cendres d'un braçat de llenya,
i els ossos —que orgullosos que eren!:   ossos
nus no són gaire diferents
0840 dels d'una carcassa de gos—,
sense l'abric de carn i pell,
s'assemblen tant als caramells
que pengen, esmolats, de teules
o de la boca d'una gàrgola
0845 a l'hora que, encesos pel sol
de mig matí, veiem que estan
a punt de començar-se a fondre!

Com és sagrat, el nostre cos!   cos
Com la muntanya o com el riu,
0850 com el boscatge o com la neu.
Sagrat, tot i que es va marcint.
Tot i que es fa malbé, sagrat
(potser per'xò encara ho és més).
Per bé que sota el sol dels anys
0855 vagi enfosquint-se, i se li arrugui
el front com una pell de fruita,
i encara que els cabells li caiguin

green boughs on the air, pines and oaks,
and the black that greys the sides of
0830   the rocky slate that is crumbling
under the hefty weight of time.
But that, in death, we made dust as
white as that of the track on which
I tread. But that all of our bones
0835   were made up of bright porphyry!
When burned, the body bears dust, grey
like the cinders from firewood trunks,
and the bones: how proud they once were!   BONES
Naked not so different from
0840   those of the carcass of some dog
without the wrap of flesh and skin,
they seem so like those icicles
that dangle, sharpened, from rooftops
or from the mouth of some gargoyle
0845   whilst, incandescent in the mid-
morning sun, we view them as they
sit at the moment of melting!

How sacred they are, our bodies!   BODY
Like the mountain or the river,
0850   like the woodland or the snowflake.
Sacred, despite its withering.
Sacred, despite its weaknesses
(perhaps more so because of this).
Though the years under the sun do
0855   darken it, and its brow wrinkles
up like the peel of a fruit and
despite its hair falling away

o es tornin de color de plata.
Pensava tot això en una època
en què resol tanta de gent
fer-se gravar la pell (¿potser
creuen merèixer-se un cos únic?
¿De debò els cal, per sentir això,
el recurs a un burí entintat?):
dibuixos i paraules, signes,
i de vegades arabescos
que formen lletges gelosies,
enrevessades teranyines,
per no deixar veure nu l'ésser.
Conviu, sovint, el tatuatge
amb ferro —anella, pistó, creu—
clavat allà on hi ha un moll de carn
—orella, llengua, llavi, nas,
melic o cella—, i aleshores
el cos s'assembla a una d'aquelles
peces de cuiro dels basters
que han d'acabar formant la sella.
Heus aquí el cos tot decorat
del nostre temps —antany només
duien argolles i arracades
els fers pirates de novel·la,
i sols els llops de mar es feien
gravar el nom d'una dona al braç—;
avui, però, s'ha omplert de cop
el nostre món d'aquests marins
de l'alt secà amb el seu llast d'àncores
i imitadors de futbolistes—,

0860
0865
0870
0875
0880
0885

or turning silver in colour.
I pondered all this in an age
0860 when the aim of so many folk
is to adorn their skin – might they
feel they deserve to be unique?
Do they really need, to this end,
the scratch of a tinted spike? – with
0865 drawings and words, signs and at times
the shapes of Arabic letters,
fashioning ugly resentment
and complicated cobwebs so
to hide away the naked self.
0870 Oft they cohabit, the tattoo
and wrought iron – ring, piston, cross –
fixed there on some morsel of flesh:
an ear, a tongue, a lip, a nose,
belly button or eyebrow 'til
0875 the body seems but one of those
examples of saddlers' leather,
still waiting to become a seat.
Gaze upon the body of our
times full adorned: in days gone by
0880 it but bore the bands and trinkets
of pirates in novels, while oft
the salty sea dogs would have girls'
names tattooed into their forearms.
Today, though, our world is forthwith
0885 filled brimming with these landlubbing
seafarers and their ballast of
anchors and those imitation

pell tatuada, perforada
la carn, un cos que hem profanat
0890 (i ànimes —tantes— avortades,
muntanyes d'ànimes de saldo
que a mi em recorden munts de roba
—barreig de peces i de talles—
a les parades d'un mercat).
0895 Abstret en dèries gens abstractes,
he ensopegat amb un sortint
de roca al meu camí, una pedra
que fa una mena de graó
enfonsat en la terra, i veig,
0900 per primer cop, en alçar el cap
tot redreçant-me, a menys de cent
gambades, rere els sis xiprers,
la meva ermita, el blanc de calç
a la façana restaurada,
0905 els contraforts, als laterals,
rocam que neix del fonament
antic, feixuc de temps i fosc
de terra, pedra del meu lloc,
pedra en què avui grana el meu ésser   ÉSSER
0910 (aquest meu ésser que, de noi,
només sabia de lliscar-hi
igual que l'aigua de la pluja),
tan diferent de la que extreuen
al veïnatge d'Alcover,
0915 que té la netedat d'un llenç
quan una punta de carbó
no ha començat encara a fer-hi

footballers, their tattooed skin and
perforated flesh, a body
0890 desecrated by us — and so
many miscarried souls, mountains
of loose spirits like piles of clothes,
a mix of outfits and sizes,
all heaped up on the market stalls.
0895 Engrossed in faintly abstract whims,
I've stumbled on a jutting ridge
of rock in the midst of my way,
a stone that forms a style of step
into the soil sunk. And I see
0900 for the first time, raising my head
and standing up straight, fewer than
a hundred strides off and behind
six cypress trees, my hermitage:
the white of the façade, revived
0905 in lime, the buttresses on the
sides, rubble born of the ancient
foundations, heavy with time and
dark with earth, homely old pebbles,
rock that today grinds my being   BEING
0910 – this being of mine that, as a
boy, knew nothing more than to slip
and slither like rainwater –, so
distinct to that which they extract
from the Alcover neighbourhood,
0915 with its purity of linen
before a sharpened carbon point
is yet to start marking out the

els primers traços d'un dibuix,
i abans que cap pinzell no hi deixi
0920 —moll de pintura— el regalim
concret de siluetes i ombres;
pedra, també, tan diferent
d'aquella roja, com d'argila,
que va servir, al poble de Prades,
0925 per fer la font, l'església, cases...
Enfilo, doncs, el darrer tram
del meu camí, i, com més a prop
em sé del lloc que vull atènyer,
més sento abissar-me en el temps
0930 en què el marrec el descobria
i el jove hi anava a llegir.
Parlo d'uns anys en què l'ermita,
fita inestable a la muntanya,
semblava estar esperant, inerme,
0935 l'hora del seu esllavissall,
aquell segon en què es consuma
l'estrèpit sord d'una ruïna;
anys sense culte i sense mica
de foc que crema, agònic brot
0940 d'espelmes i de ciris, vida
encesa, vida que s'amorta,
flors que regalen i es panseixen,
flor de les ombres (cera i ble,
tija i corol·la), anys de finestres
0945 franques de vidre en què els ocells,
amb els seus nius i cants, devien
senyorejar la nau deserta,

first vague traces of a drawing,
before a paintbrush soft with paint
0920   leaves on it that particular
trickle of silhouettes and shades.
Rock, too, oh so different from
that reddish earth, clay, for instance,
once used in the town of Prades
0925   to build the fountain, church and homes.
And so I follow the last slip
of my path and the closer I
get to the place I want to be,
the more joined do I feel to the
0930   time when the boy first discovered
and the youth was starting to read.
I refer to the years when the
hermitage, that fitful bluff cairn,
seemed to be waiting, defenceless,
0935   for the hour of its sliding crash,
that split-second when it's consumed
by the deafening racket of
ruin: years without cult or scraps
of burning fire, agonising
0940   buds of wax candles, searing life,
existence burning itself out,
withering gifts of stale flowers,
the flower in the shadows – wax
and wick, pedicel and petal –,
0945   years of empty panes in which birds,
with their eyries and song, no doubt
held sway in the deserted hall,

qui sap si els porcs senglars també
—aterrada la porta— en feien
0950 —feres seglars, natura nòmada—
un aixopluc per hores fredes
per no haver de parar, llom nus,
el calabruix que ve del cel
i per no haver de petjar el glaç
0955 damunt la terra de l'hivern.
¿Hi havia un Crist desemparat,   CRIST
llavors, amb la corona —al front—
d'espines, cos morent, i un plor
que regalima com la sang
0960 d'una llançada, el plor de l'home,
més bleïdor que cera ardent,
l'home crucificat, pesant,
al fons de l'absis, en la fosca,
l'home implorant, que avarament
0965 aferra els seus dos claus (va escriure-ho,
en un bell vers terrible, Ritsos)?   RITSOS
Crist a la creu, nàufrag i fusta
en l'oceà de l'univers,
l'estesa densa i brogidora
0970 sense la vora d'una platja,
sense el perfil verd d'una costa,
perquè és tot aigua i no hi ha terra,
tot aigua fosca, espessa i fonda,
i no hi ha límit ni vorada,
0975 no hi ha frontera, no hi ha terme,
i no es fa peu si no és amb una
feixuga llosa d'aigua al cap.

and who could know if wild boars, too,
the door burst and toppled, once took
0950 – secular beasts, nature's nomad –
shelter there during the cold hours
so as not to stop (knotted loin)
in the hail falling from the skies
and to avoid walking the ice
0955 cloaking cold the wintery Earth.
Was there then an abandoned Christ,   CHRIST
topped by his crown, infamous on
his brow, a languishing god, tears
trickling on down like the blood brought
0960 forth by the lance, the tears of man,
blazing hotter than scorching wax,
man crucified, slumped down at the
nethermost of the void, in gloom,
the man imploring, who, lurching,
0965 grasps at his two nails? Was this penned
(a verse of dread grace) by Ritsos?   RITSOS
Christ shipwrecked on the cross and wood
on the sea of the universe,
that dense, deafening expansion
0970 lacking the seashore of the beach,
without the green form of the coast,
being all water and no land,
dark water all, heavy and deep,
without limit, without border,
0975 there is no frontier and no end,
no touching the bottom without
a crushing burden of water

Ara he envellit: la meva cara,
les meves mans han envellit
0980   com el diari que quedava
tot un matí exposat al sol,
i penso en Jesucrist, tan jove,
de cos atlètic, malferit,
i en la mirada que ens confia
0985   feresa humana i solitud
—l'ull dolençós sota el front greu
en un cap acalat, vençut—
i, en ascendir pel tram final
del meu camí, m'acaro amb ell
0990   en el record, reveig el seu
davallament, les diligències
sagrades de desfer-li el llaç
estret dels claus contra la fusta,
d'alliberar-lo d'aquell llast
0995   de la natura moridora,
i els ulls de Crist són dues brases
que avui m'escalfen l'embalbida
pell d'un cor cec, braser dels ulls
que fa com el mercuri líquid
1000   dels vells termòmetres trencats:
de nens, solíem esclafar-ne
—el tou d'un dit tan excitable—
la gota desencapsulada,
color de plata, que es tornava
1005   màgicament a recompondre.
Absort en pensaments tan varis,
sento, de cop, una olor d'aura

overhead. I've grown old: my face,
my hands have waned, grown decrepit
0980 like a newspaper that has spent
the morning sitting in the sun.
And I think of Jesus Christ, so
youthful, athletic, cruelly maimed,
and of the gaze that grants us our
0985 human despair and loneliness
– that ailing eye under the grave
brow of a hanging head, beaten –
and, climbing the final section
of my path, I encounter him
0990 in my memories, see again
his downfall, the sacred vigour
of unfastening the tight knot
of nails from within the timber,
freeing him from that burden of
0995 nature's cosmic mortality,
and Christ's eyes are two red embers
that today warm the numb skin of
my arid heart, a bonfire of
eyes, aping liquid mercury
1000 in old, broken thermometers.
As children, oft would we heat up
– a restless finger's fleshy pad –
the un-encapsulated drop,
silver in colour, that regrouped
1005 magically time and again.
Engrossed in various concerns,
I forthwith detect the scent of

de Crist en una mata seca
de farigola que he burxat
1010 amb la punta d'un peu, o el veig
en la pols lleu del meu camí,
que el sol emblanca tantes hores
—un marge blanc en aquest llibre   LLIBRE
brogent de la naturalesa—.
1015 Si fos el temps de primavera,
potser se'm faria present,
ben a tocar de casa, en camps
plens d'una infinitat d'espigues
de blat excitades pel vent
1020 —cotes de malla verdes, ínfimes,
innúmer esquadró del tros—,
al mes d'abril, quan remou l'hora
—molla de pluges i de saba—
l'arrel més fonda de la terra,
1025 el sentiment del nostre viure
i la brancada de la sang.
I penso que l'adolescent
que vaig ser un dia acostumava
a fer equivaldre la ruïna
1030 de la modesta esglesiola
amb la del cos crucificat.
¿Potser creuré, de nou, un dia?,   CREURE
¿he cregut mai?, ¿què vol dir creure?,
¿ho fa d'una semblant manera,
1035 tothom qui creu? Creure i pensar,
¿s'arribaran a trobar mai?
(Crist ha ofegat un crit, que el tall

Christ's aura in a dry thicket
of thyme that I have prodded at
1010   with the tip of my foot, or I
see the slight dust of the pathway
that the sun spends hours whitening.
A white margin from this book that   BOOK
comes roaring out of the landscape.
1015   If it were but springtime weather,
I might be more aware of it,
so close to home, in full pastures
of immeasurable sheaves of
wheat, murmuring in the zephyr
1020   – crowns of ignoble green chainmail,
an innumerable squadron
at once – of this April month when
comes the hour, moist from rain and sap,
the deepest essence of this earth,
1025   sentiment of our existence
and the bloodied blooming branchlet.
And I think of how the young man
I once was before so often
associated the ruin
1030   of that modest sanctuary
with that of its crucified frame.
Will I one day believe again?   BELIEVE
Have I ever believed? What does
'believe' mean? Do all believers
1035   trust in the same way? Belief and
thought, will ever the two connect?
Christ has swallowed a cry, the cuts

de la punta dels claus li esqueixa
la carn dels peus i de les mans
1040 i, fondo, li n'estella els ossos
—peus recollits en un sol clau:
feixucs, marcits, donats a mort;
i, en canvi, mans, en l'esbatec
de l'aire, ofertes per renéixer—.
1045 Gemega Crist, i encara tremen
els fonaments del nostre món.)

Segueixo amunt, i ja no trobo
sinó el gruix tou de la pols blanca
sota els meus peus, el blau translúcid
1050 d'un cel velat per la calitja,
i aquell coixí del verd dels pins
i dels avellaners, més fosc,
ça i lla, pacientment vivint
en la seva ànima de planta.
1055 Ara reparo en una pedra   PEDRA
de marge cantonera: hi veig
un rastre de color, ditades
d'un roig com de rovell de sang.
Ha de ser l'obra de la mà
1060 d'algú que s'hi ha posat —ferida
la pell per una esgarrinxada—,
perquè no sembla pas pintura
ni hi reconec cap signe o lletra.
¿Quan deu haver sigut que algú
1065 ha reposat, dits ensagnats,
damunt el passamà dels rocs?
¿És sang del dia o tot va ocórrer

from the nail ends dig deep into
the flesh of his feet and hands: they
1040   chip at the bones inside his feet,
both bound by a single rivet,
gross, shrunken, forsaken to death.
His hands, though, are beating in the
breeze, ready for his renaissance.
1045   Christ moans, and still the foundations
of our world tremble and shudder.

I go onwards, encountering
nothing but the soft clots of white
dust under my feet, the thin sky,
1050   translucent blue and veiled by haze,
and that green cushion of pine and
hazelnut trees, still darker and
dotted here and there, patiently
existing in their plant-like souls.
1055   Now I stop and stare at a stone   STONE
on the rocky margin. I see
a dash of colour, fingerprints
of a bloody-red yolk colour.
Plainly cruor of the person's
1060   hand that placed it there – a wounded
epidermis, scratched deep and scarred –,
it surely not being paint, and
no sign nor letter do I see.
When must it have been, the act of
1065   placing it, fingers all bloodied,
upon that stony bannister?
Is it today's blood? Or did it

fa més d'un any, quan es degué
ferir algun vell, buscant espàrrecs,
1070 i hi recolzà una mà, cercant
amb l'altra, lliure, un mocador
dins la butxaca? ¿I si ja és mort,
perquè era un home que, potser,
queia sovint en caminar
1075 pel bosc, tot enfilant senders,
un d'aquells jaios caparruts
que tresquen sols i sense por
de la foscor o bé de les bèsties,
un d'aquells tipus que no temen
1080 ni l'ombra de la mort ni els altres,
i no fan cas a Déu ni als homes,
i parà el cop amb la mà nua
damunt la brossa, arran de soques,
punxent com escampall de vidres?
1085 ¿O, tal vegada, aquesta taca
és sols un color estrany que ha fet
la pedra al cap de moltes dècades,
potser l'herència d'una etapa
del tot perduda en la memòria:
1090 ombra en un roc que algun pagès
va desvetllar del son, colgat
a terra, per posar-lo al cap-
damunt del marge, merlet tosc?

Aquest és l'últim repetjó
1095 que ha d'emmenar-me a lloc. Ja albiro
—formació escarida— els sis
xiprers de tronc i brancam secs

happen a year or more gone when
some old man was hurt, hunting for
1070   asparagus, and put his hand
there, grasping with the other for
the handkerchief in his pocket?
And if he is already dead,
being a man who, perhaps, fell
1075   often on his way to the woods,
trailing paths, one of those stubborn
old men who would wander alone,
fearing not the darkness or beasts,
one of those who is daunted not
1080   by the shadow of death or else,
and who takes no notice of God
or men, stopping his fall with his
bare hand upon the brush, touching
the trunks, thorny like broken glass?
1085   Or perhaps this stain is just a
curious colour taken on
by the rock over long decades?
Perhaps a hand-me-down from an
era long since lost to the world?
1090   A shadow on a rock that some
farmer once dozed upon, resting
on the ground, placed on the top of
the bank, a clumsy battlement?

This is the final brisk ascent
1095   to lead me to the place. I have
before me bare, shorn formations,
the six dry, bare-branched cypress trees   CYPRESS TREES

(xiprer: hospitalitat i auguri).
I se'm destaca el blanc de calç
1100 a la façana restaurada.
Sento desig de fer descalç
el darrer tram del meu camí
fins a tocar la portalada
de fusta vella de l'ermita
1105 i, abans, l'escorça d'aquell pi
en què un migdia quedà inscrita,
sota la punta de burí
d'una navalla que tenia
—com si fos pàgina o papir—,
1110 la joia juvenil d'uns noms,
memòria d'una amor proscrita.
(Ningú no grava els noms d'amor
en una escorça de xiprer.
A diferència dels pollancres,
1115 dels àlbers, plàtans o moreres,
que són de tronc més clar i més llis,
els pins, d'una arrugada escorça,
no que no fan de bon escriure-hi,
bé que el que dic, sota un avís
1120 després —un rètol de perill
d'incendis, o potser el d'una àrea
privada de cacera— havia
format un breu requadre net,
com repujat, on vaig inscriure
1125 un nom de noia sobre el meu.)
Emperò el temps, amb la insolència
de qui combat amb els soldats

(the cypress: warmth and good omens).
And I am struck by the chalky
1100 whiteness of the now restored front.
I feel the urge to walk the last
part of my way barefoot until
I reach the venerable old
entryway of the hermitage
1105 and, before, the bark of that pine
on which one midday was written,
under the point of a cutting
edge I once carried, as if on
paper or parchment, the precious
1110 teenage treasure of sundry names,
memories of illicit love.
Nobody engraves lovers' names
in the rough barks of cypress trees.
Unlike the poplars, the plane trees
1115 or mulberries, all of which are
of smoother, starker trunks to touch,
cypress trees, with their wrinkled barks,
do not lend themselves to be marked,
despite what I say, sat later
1120 under a placard of wildfire
warnings or perhaps a private
hunting sign that had before then
engendered a clean, fleeting box,
almost embossed, where I inscribed
1125 a girl's name on top of my own.
But time, with the insolence of
those who do battle with the most

més ferms que són els de l'oblit,
va esborrar els mots esgrafiats,
1130 que avui són menys que un fil, encara,
de serradures sota el tall
dentat de plata d'un xerrac.
Reposarà la mà en el tronc,   PI
i pensaré que els nostres noms
1135 —escrits amb la cal·ligrafia
de tremp grosser d'una navalla—
han escalfat durant molts anys
la saba d'aquest pi que ajuda
a fer, damunt el lloc, una ombra
1140 més densa i més de bon estar-hi,
més agraïda que aquella altra
tan abrinada dels xiprers
que repta fins a projectar-se
damunt l'hostal soliu de l'ànima.
1145 Tants anys després, és com si encara
pogués sentir-me al cap dels dits
la densa llàgrima aromada
de la resina, un moc de pols...

I faig, descalç, els darrers passos,
1150 i bé que, a còpia d'anys, els peus
sembla que duguin un abric
molt més de crosta que de pell,
sento la calda de la terra
—com si sentís l'activitat
1155 febril d'un forn sota el meu pis,
pel qual, peunú, anés caminant
insomne o, fins i tot, somnàmbul,

unshakeable soldiers, those of
neglect, erased the engraved names,
1130 nowadays nothing more than a
few carved lines from the serrated
scratch of a silver handsaw blade.
My hand will settle on the trunk,   PINE TREE
and I will contemplate our names,
1135 written with the calligraphy
of a knife's coarse promontory,
how they warmed, for many years, the
sap of this pine that now works to
cast a shadow over this place,
1140 making it denser, more pleasant,
more generous than that other
shade, thin and gaunt, from the cypress
trees that fight to project themselves
above the church, lone and silent.
1145 So many years after, it's as
if I can still feel under touch
the thick, aromatic teardrops
of the dusty resin mucus.

And, barefooted, I take the last
1150 few steps, and again and again
over the years my feet seem to
bear a covering more of crust
than of skin, I feel the heat of
the earth as if sensing the slight
1155 heat of an oven below my
flat, in which, unshod, I wandered
sleeplessly or even sleepwalked

en hores de la matinada—,
i sento el sol, empolsegat,
1160 en el camí que ara arroenta
(i sento, encara —despullats
els peus, i, en gran mesura, l'ésser—,
més fondament el pas que faig;
el món, llavors, gairebé em cou,
1165 perquè és tot fet de pols de brases;
però, al voltant del cor, regala,
en forma d'aigua —un doll constant
d'aigua de font tan fresca i blava—).
Pel cel, ben net de núvols, fuig,
1170 desfent-se, un rastre d'avió
—fil blanc d'una puntada al buit—.
¿Filen, les Moires? ¿Mai sargeixen?
La rúbrica, en el llenç celeste,
s'esborrarà abans que jo toqui
1175 amb la mà esquerra l'estuc nou
de la façana de l'ermita
(amagadís, també, o equívoc,
signa l'autor del que és creat).
Coronaré aquests últims metres
1180 molt més a poc a poc: he après
a demorar l'instant segur
del meu plaer abans de gaudir-ne
(una manera com una altra
de fotre's de la fi de tot,
1185 i de pensar que és un mateix
el qui comanda el propi temps).
La terra acull arrels, la terra   TERRA

in the early hours of the day.
And I feel the arenose sun
1160   on the path that now twists and turns
– and I feel in my feet and to
a large degree, my spirit, both
naked, nude, the path underfoot.
The world, then, almost burns me up,
1165   formed as it is of soot and ash.
But around my heart, it offers,
like water, a constant cascade
of spring water, fresh, crisp and blue.
In the now cloudless sky, vapour
1170   trails from aeroplanes drift away:
white wires pointing to nothingness.
Do the Fates ever spin, ever
darn? The rubric, in that linen
firmament, will vanish before
1175   I place my left hand on the new
stucco of the hermitage face
(the creator's seal has since been
hidden from view, too, or misplaced).
I will crown these last few metres
1180   at a much slower rate: I've learned
to prolong the assured instance
of my bliss ere relishing it
– just another way of laughing
at the sum of it all, seeing
1185   it as one and the same person,
he who manages his own time.
The earth collects our roots, the earth   EARTH

collirà el fruit del nostre cos
quan sigui prou madur per caure
1190 —¿fins quan, el meu, verdejarà
encara?, ¿i quan serà que els sucs
de mort —aquell ferment d'un vi
danyós— es deuran fer prou dolços
dintre la polpa del meu cor
1195 per fer-ne verolar la pell
i, poc després, deixar que pengi
—única fruita, el cor, podrida
que ha de servir només per péixer
ocells i enllaminir les mosques—
1200 de la branca fruital, a punt
d'esqueixar-se, del pit del tors
del cos de l'ànima sencera
—misèria de la nostra vida?
I penso tot això, i componc
1205 de cor uns versos que em caldrà
fixar al paper en arribar a casa
(no he fet servir gens la llibreta;
n'esbosso, però, el nucli, l'ham
d'una paraula lluminosa,
1210 damunt la pàgina de pols
del meu camí, que he anat seguint
més aviat com si es tractés
de desplegar, morós, un rotlle,
una escriptura discursiva).
1215 De cop, reparo en una cosa
que hi ha a la vora del camí:
m'hi acosto i veig una desferra,

will harvest the fruits of our limbs,
once mature enough to plummet.
1190   How long will my own still endure?
And when will the juices of death,
that fermentation of harmful
wine, no doubt fully sweet enough
within the poultice of my heart
1195   to bring up colour to my skin
and, shortly after, allow it
to hang. The heart, that rare, rotten
fruit that serves for naught but to feed
birds and to seduce greedy flies
1200   to the fruit-bearing branch, ready
to slip the core of the body's
torso, the spirit absolute:
the misery of our being?
And I ponder this, composing
1205   by heart some verses that I should
put down on paper back at home.
I have used no sort of notebook.
I sketch, however, the centre,
the grapnel of some shining word
1210   upon the dusty page of the
pathway that I have long followed
as if, most likely, it was to
sluggishly spread on out, rolling,
like some meandering scripture.
1215   Forthwith, I fix eyes on something
sitting on the edge of the track.
I approach and spy some remains,

"une charogne infâme". Més
modesta que la del poema,
1220   fema un ermot. Aquí no hi ha,
però, cap predador esperant
que jo me'n vagi per tornar
a alimentar-s'hi, profanant-la.
Que poc que en queda, de l'antiga
1225   carcassa —¿de quin animal?,
un gat cerval, potser—: hi ha un os
que apunta sota un tou de pèl
—que es va esqueixar per poder extreure
la carn nutrícia del cos
1230   inerme, bategant, pletòric—,
i encara mitja dentadura
—¿de quina salvatgina?, ¿és una
rabosa, com se'n diu als Ports?—
en un musell mal descarnat
1235   —parany esgavellat, inútil—.
¿Et reconeixes —em pregunto—
en les despulles de la bèstia?
¿T'hi reconeixes com has fet,
de sempre, en la rosella efímera
1240   que fa brandar la pinzellada
del seu color, i que tant celebres
de veure sanguejar en el verd
dels marges del país, dels marges
del temps incipient d'estiu?
1245   Prat verd, ordi madur, hemorràgia.

I ja soc dalt, davant mateix
de la portada de l'ermita.

CARRONYA

'*une charogne infâme.*' So much more   CARRION
modest than that of the poem:
1220   a clod of a corpse. Here there is,
though, no predator waiting for
me to leave so as to return
to its feast, to desecrate it.
How little remains of the tired
1225   carcass. And from which animal?
A lynx, perhaps. A bone protrudes
from under the downy pelage
that was slipped aside to extract
the salubrious flesh of the
1230   helpless, beating, cascading frame,
still displaying half gnawed teeth marks.
From which savage beast? Is it a
rabosa, as they say in Ports?
There is a half-eaten snout, too:
1235   a useless, disjointed gin trap.
Do you see yourself, I wonder,
in the leftovers of the beast?
Do you see there that which always
you see in the fleeting poppy
1240   that inspires brandished brushstrokes of
the colour you so revel in,
seeing the green verges of the
countryside bleed red with the hems
of the early days of summer?
1245   Green field, mature corn, haemorrhage.

I've reached the top and stand before
the entrance to the hermitage

Em sento alliberat del feix
llenyós dels anys. Toco la fita
1250 de guix·de la façana. Sec
en el pedrís. He vist la cua
d'un esquirol, i sento un crec
de dents contra una closca crua.
(La trona, en la branca de pi,
1255 i l'ocupant, que no hi predica:
adelerat, rosega un bri,
gra d'or que el nodreix una mica
—de nit, seria un ratpenat—.)
La cua fa com una flama
1260 que penja, inversa, del forcat
amb un color agostat de rama.
Ara m'aixeco del pedrís,
m'arribo fins a la barana:
des d'aquí dalt veig un país
1265 aturonat, la vasta plana
que mor al mar, alguns barrancs,
el foc de la refineria
(i un fum malsà), polígons blancs,
el nyap d'una deixalleria.
1270 Perquè és també el país del temps
—la terra de la meva vida—,
la mort el va adobant amb fems
de bells records, i du garfida
la forca d'enfonsar al femer,
1275 no pas la dalla de la sega.
Hi veig, ubèrrim, un graner,
i arreu brillar l'aigua que rega.

and I feel free of the woody
weight of years. I touch the stucco
1250   milestone on the façade and sit
on the stony bench. I see a
squirrel's tail and hear the crack of
its teeth against a raw nutshell.
It is devoured on a pine branch.
1255   The occupant, wasting no time,
gnaws at the nut, a nourishing
drop of gold dust, passionately
– by night-time, it would be a bat.
His tail flickers like a flame that
1260   hangs, inverted, from a poker,
painted colours like August boughs.
I now alight my stony shelf
and I come to the balustrade:
from here on high I see a land
1265   of rolling hills, the vast plateau
running down to the sea, some cliffs,
the fire from a refinery
and its fetid fumes, white business
zones and the stain of a landfill.
1270   For it is, too, a land of time.
The motherland of my lifetime.
Death enriches it with the dung
of good memories and clenches
the compost heap pitchfork tightly
1275   rather than use the reapers' scythe.
I see a bursting granary,
and shining water all around.

El poble avui s'ha fet més gran: POBLE
al tros d'ahir, hi ha una parcel·la,
1280   i, allà on l'hort verdejava, hi han
—cel·la al costat d'una altra cel·la—
bastit, tallades pel mateix
patró, unes cases adossades.
Aquí, un centre logístic creix
1285   (de moment, sols parets alçades).
Tot això és nou. Però el vessant
més obagós de la muntanya
—feixes que baixen fins arran
de la riera, on no s'afanya,
1290   des de fa mesos, l'aigua— és ben
semblant al de tants anys enrere.
Algunes canyes. Corre el vent
pel llit polsós de la riera.
Es deu morir, exhaust, a l'indret
1295   —l'umbracle— de la Font dels Gossos.   FONT
Recer, a l'hivern, humit i fred,
roures antics que són esbossos
de pilars vius del paradís.
Qui sap si allà, dins la canella,
1300   l'aigua fa un raig o un degotís,
si és boca morta o cantarella.
També aquí dalt l'aigua es fa doll
—humil— de font: hi ha una fornícula
de pedra que el resguarda. Un toll
1305   per pica. No el treball agrícola,
sinó la set del caminant
és el destí de la font closa.

The village today is bigger: VILLAGE
in that part was a piece of land,
1280 and there, where the garden once grew
green, there are, plot bordering plot,
buildings cut from the same pattern
 and a few semi-detached homes.
Here, a warehouse centre now grows
1285 (currently, just some standing walls).
All this is new. But the darkest
aspects of the mountainous slopes,
parallel shelves that tumble down
to the torrent where for months now
1290 water does not run, are the same
as it has been for many years.
Some lone reeds. The wind blows lightly
across the dusty riverbed.
No doubt it dies, exhausted, at
1295 the shaded Font dels Gossos spring.   SPRING
In winter it runs, cold and damp,
along ancient oaks, sketches of
living pillars of paradise.
Who knows if, there, within the spouts,
1300 the water flows or slowly drips,
if it's dead or alive down there?
Up here, too, the water trickles
humbly from the fountain: there is
a stone font that stores it. A cup
1305 for a sink. The wayfarer's thirst,
in lieu of fuel for the fields, is
the lonely fount's destination.

Omplo una embosta d'aigua. M'han
quedat —vessen damunt la llosa
1310   les mans—, igual que els solcs d'un hort
que es tornen riu de cop, negades
les línies: lletra ema (¿mort?)
o dues ves entrellaçades
(¿vida?), de cap per'vall. Antany,
1315   amb l'amenaça de ruïna,
l'ermita era una llar del plany
—vida que es pon, mort que matina—.
Ara, de lluny, pot semblar un mas,
un d'aquells nobles casalicis:
1320   si havia anat a mal borràs,
es dreça avui, sota els auspicis
de l'ànima avial del lloc,
com l'orgullosa barbacana
que aguanta ferma. Evoco el roc
1325   que fulla —escriu—, floreix i grana
—J. V. Foix, del seu país—.   FOIX
No sé per què em ve a la memòria:
el roc se'ns torna engrunadís,
sempre encalçant la pròpia història.
1330   M'estimo més concebre un cel
de fosca nit, florit d'estrelles.
I em sento a punt de llevar el vel
que, com la pell d'unes parpelles,
impenetrable, enfosqueix l'ull
1335   real, secret, de cada cosa.
Baldament sigui de reüll
—alçada la feixuga llosa

I clasp my hands full of water.
It moves, flowing over layers
on my palms, like the wake over
land that is abruptly flooded,
negating the lines. The letter
'D' (death?) or two interlinked 'L's
(life?), upside down. The year before,
under threat of total ruin,
the hermitage was a place of
sorrow: life that fades, death that swells.
Now, from far, it might look like a
Mas, one of those noble mansions.
But if it had all nigh gone wrong,
it's better today under the
aegis of the place's innate
spirit, like the proud barbican
still standing strong. 'I evoke the
rock that sprouts leaves, blooms and seeds' wrote
J.V. Foix of his own country.   FOIX
I know not why this springs to mind.
The rock itself crumbles away,
ever chasing its own fable.
I love more to gaze at the sky
in the dark of night, awash with
stars. And I am close to lifting
the veil that, like some eyelid skin,
impervious, darkens the close,
true eye at the heart of all things?
Despite it being but a glimpse,
the weighty flagstone rises up,

1310
1315
1320
1325
1330
1335

que esmorteix el batec del món
i obliga a veure-ho tot translúcid—,
1340 baldament sigui un sol segon,
amb pensament de sobte lúcid,
podria entendre què és això
que hem convingut a dir-ne vida,
si és la condemna o si és el do,
1345 si és l'arribada o la partida.
Ara mateix no em veig amb cor
d'especular. Fa tanta calda!
Neix un infant i un vell es mor
cada minut. Un obrer malda
1350 per no ofegar-se, un pagès cau
quan, enfonsant la fanga, troba,
en lloc de terra flonja, el blau
—que, descolgat, sembla una clova—
d'un casc de ferro. Sento dir,
1355 a les cigales, lletanies.
De la capçada d'algun pi
volen a la d'un altre. Dies
monòtons de l'estiu! Enyor
del cant humit de les granotes   GRANOTA
1360 en els captards d'agost, tenor
de mà pressuda que pren notes
al desbridat dictat de l'ull.
Dins l'espadanya, la campana
quieta. Fetes un embull,
1365 veig dues mosques, la membrana
d'una ala vibra. M'entretinc
en coses francament petites.

drowning out the beat of the world,
forcing it to be viewed clearly.
1340 Despite it being but a sole
second, with sudden lucid thought
I was able to see that it's
this that we've agreed to call life,
whether a blessing or a curse,
1345 the arrival or departure.
Right now, I do not have the strength
to speculate. How hot it is!
A child is born and an old man
dies every minute. A worker
1350 strives not to drown, a farmer fails
when, sinking into the mud, he
finds, instead of porous earth, the
blue tinge that, unearthed, looks like a
shell of an iron helm. I hear
1355 litanies recited to the
cicadas. From the top of the
pines they fly from one to the next.
Oh, monotonous summer days!
Nostalgia for the humid frog   FROG
1360 song in the August evenings and
a rushed hand taking notes under
the eye's unbridled watchfulness.
Within the bell-tower, the bell
lies still. Intertwined and as one,
1365 I see two flies. The membrane of
a wing vibrates. I entertain
myself with the more minute things.

De cop em sembla sentir el dring
de la campana. A misses dites
1370 arriba una formiga a un bri:
una altra ja el carretejava.
Hi va haver un temps que vaig obrir
la porta d'una estança blava.
La noia duia un vestit clar
1275 que feia un estampat d'espiga.
Però, batall tocatardà
o ressaguer com la formiga,
no vaig arribar a l'hora al cor.
No em facis perdre el temps, memòria!
1380 Eren de llauna i semblen d'or,
els dies compartits, escòria!

CAMPANA

Torno a baixar, tants anys després,
sol, de l'ermita de Sant Pere.
De cop, tot pren un nou carés.
1385 Res no mereix la nostra espera
sinó el xerric del primer grill
o la improbable aigua d'un xàfec.
Proposa un viure més senzill,
el meu poema. Lluny del tràfec
1390 del món d'avui, d'un entrellat
revés. Falta la signatura
del manuscrit. ¿És llast o esclat?
¿Terrejarà, esdevindrà altura?

I ja m'acosto a l'últim vers
1395 d'aquesta *Ermita* narrativa.

I think I hear the abrupt ring
of the bell. Later in the day   BELL
1370   an ant arrives at a morsel:
another has since lifted it
away. There was a time when I
once opened the door to a blue
bedroom. The girl wore a bright dress
1375   stamped with the shape of a corn sheaf.
But like the belated clapper
or the tardy path of the ant,
I arrived to her heart too late.
Oh, waste not my time, memory!
1380   They were of tin, but seemed of gold,
the days once shared, now but debris!

Anew I descend, years after,
lone, from Sant Pere's hermitage.
All suddenly assumes new forms.
1385   Naught deserves our attention but
the chirping of the first cricket
or the improbable downpour.
My poem proposes a more
simple life. Far from the bustle
1390   of the modern world, the lack of
insight. The manuscript lacks an
ending. A burden or a blast?
Will it flounder or will it soar?

And I come now to the last verse
1395   of this *Hermitage* narrative.

Si ha de pesar o se l'endú el cerç,
si mor o ha de romandre viva,
no ho sap ningú! Jo me'n desprenc:
els versos són la meva herència.   HERÈNCIA
1400   Llibre a través, com per un trenc,
flueix la sang de l'existència.

(Vilafranca del Penedès, maig del 2015 – juny del 2016)

If it weighs heavy or is born
away on the wind, lives or dies,
no one can know! I leave you now:
these verses are my legacy.   LEGACY
1400   Running through a book, like a crack,
the blood of existence flows free.

(Vilafranca del Penedès, May, 2015 – June, 2016)

The Pomegranate Tree

For Susanna

The first time he noticed the pomegranate tree was the day he came across one of its fruits lying in his path. The track itself was all fine white sand and dust and so the brightly coloured fruit was easy to spot. Lifting up his head, he saw other pomegranates still hanging tentatively onto the branches like petite water droplets waiting to hurl themselves down off some shingle roof.

The pomegranate was half agape as if someone had tried to force it open. Some of the arils — translucent, red-fleshed and seeded — were dirty from the dust. The lonely fruit was but a solitary mouth, ripped out of a body and left lying on the ground, browbeaten and humiliated. The walker had always found that pomegranate arils made him think of cathedral stained-glass windows. But now, seeing the open-mouthed fruit lying in the dust, its bottom lip running up against its teeth, he thought sooner of the filthy, dust encrusted glass of some small attic porthole. While still on the tree, mature and entire, fruit can evoke heady dreams of celestial bodies and great heights. Green apples, for example, cut out against a twilight-blue sky, form small autumnal planetary systems in the mind's eye. He wrote down *poma granada a terra* in the small notebook he was carrying.

He kicked at the fruit and it somersaulted away like some small, half-dead animal flailing across the floor, its body out of control. There is a signpost behind the pomegranate tree that points towards the forest where the man was headed: a simple place name and a distance of two point three kilometres. The sign is slightly taller than the tree but the plant's greenery adorns the metal pole, bedecking it in foliage. Perhaps they erected the sign on a day when the pomegranate tree was bare and leafless; all winter austerity, pricked by the white air. Perhaps a while ago the austere signpost and the tree's bare branches kept their distance from each other before growing closer together. Perhaps the appearance of leaves has brought about a little more hospitality than the naked branch or the old tree's skeleton. Because along the verge where the pomegranate tree proudly stood, seemingly escorted by its signpost, everything else was even and low: the fields of barley; the flattish path itself; the vineyards with their bushy vines that tend to shrink under their own thick foliage. And so the man sat down with his back against the tree trunk and looked up to admire the imperfect roundness of the fruits above him, coloured like light pouring in through cathedral stained-glass windows. The living pomegranates on the bough. The arils within the pomegranates. The seeds within the arils. All of it spoke of life and death within the mouth.

When out summer walking, the man often sees pigeons quenching their thirst in farmhouse water butts. There are thirsty bees too, that repeatedly tickle the standing water. Some of them float dead on the surface: their thirst has driven them to their deaths. They weigh little more than the sliver of feather that the pigeon has shed. The water is full of life and death.

A stream of water from a subterranean source — a mine, perhaps — spews out into the overflowing butt. What patience that water has!

The man walks and reads, every now and then lifting up his head from the white pages and black letters in front of him. He has occasionally suffered unpleasant surprises: tens of turtledoves hidden within the branches of an almond tree, perhaps hoping to crack open the green cases of the almonds that are forming in their shells, or pecking at the sparse grains of an old wheat sheaf, wizened and dry in perpetuity like a dead man's three day old beard (or relative perpetuity, at least — until the beard and the adjoining cheeks melt away into the skull like butter). Passing them on the path, the birds take to flight *en masse*, bewildered and perhaps fearful of the hunters' precise, leisure-time gunpowder.

> The clash of so many wings,
> That busy, alate racket
> –as if suddenly, by chance,
> a corpse had risen up from
> his grave– they scare the walker
> and pull quickly at his heart.
> He was thinking of a prayer

for a young child who had died:
if it might be said in a
thundering voice, that of beasts
– those who still care for dead flesh
and who are nourished by grass!

G eckos tend to populate the margins of the paths while
ants prefer to live on the flat.

They hide themselves, the geckos, among the rocks on the banks and slopes. There is, in the very nature of the gecko family, descendants of dragons, a deep need and desire for cover. They simultaneously long for both darkness and light.

The walker has seen a dead gecko on the path. They never die on the banks, but always on the flat. It has probably been squashed by a wheel. A wheel, that most distinguished symbol of human progress, has flattened a creature that has been in existance for a lot longer than we have.

How beautiful a living gecko really is! But dead like this, all disembowelled and dripping blood on the dusty white path, it is nothing more than a naïve final signature at the end of a tragedy. But this doesn't mean that we can't find it beautiful. This dead lizard is, in fact, even more real than the other, still slithering one. Its state of not-being is infinitely more real than that of the other's being. But what if its death came about in a different way, without being squashed? There must be many other ways for a gecko to die. Old age, perhaps? This gecko's birth from some long-forgotten egg that had once been laid on the ground was as unpredictable as its absurd death under the implacable tread of some wheel. And so it is in this sense that we are, ladies and gentlemen, not so different to geckos. Still, we crawl — perhaps never standing fully upright!

Death is the same for both men and geckos.

The walker thinks that, on his journey that day, he has already come across two victims of the human hand. A pomegranate and a gecko.

With his left hand, the man first caused evil.
He tried, then with his right, to make it good.
And what did the both of them do? The dark
or, perhaps, the light? They ruined it all.

The walker continued on his way. He followed well-worn pathways that he knew from before; from time to time he chose overgrown ones that led through copses of trees. When finding himself on one of these tracks, he usually aimed to return to the main path, though it was not always possible. And by continuing as such, purely by accident, he reached the sea. It was as if he had gone from being a mere walker and was now himself something more: a Wanderer.

The seasons changed, the weather turned and the temperature dropped. Ice sparkled on the coastal slate. A furious wind beat at the branches of a palm tree that was poking its head up over a whitewashed farmhouse fence. The wind's lugubrious voice, running along grooves or attacking any resistance it might meet, found itself abruptly subdued at the water's edge. When the Wanderer knelt down to scoop up some water, the sea, with the exception of a layer of froth, was grey in colour. A little while later, the water cleared and took on a bluer hue but when he grasped at it and cupped it in his hands, the water he saw in his palms wasn't blue, but was as transparent as the air that surrounded him.

He lay down on the pebbles. Even though it was midday, the moon was still much sharper in the sky than the sun. A black cloud that had come from the south-east started to take on different shapes in the Wanderer's mind. It only lasted some ten to twelve minutes before its dark, brooding colour, like an infected ulcer, began to lift and brighten. The first shape the cloud made in the man's eyes was that of a black cat. But the cat, like a toy that had been unstitched and emptied of fluff, quickly turned thin and scrawny, its empty skin melting away in an instant. The skin-less body that was left behind took a little while longer to disappear. Another cloud then formed a more complex image of a cross. He watched that cloudy Christ drift across the sky and trembled with emotion where he lay. Some rays of light made to cut through the body nailed to the wood, only managing to contort the scene as their strength slowly gave out.

Not long before, while he was buying sardines at a fishmonger's, the man overheard a woman talking. 'They had to bury him in a flower pit,' she said. She was talking about someone who, due to his religion, had been forbidden a burial in a Christian cemetery and so had been interred where they ditch old wreaths and withered bouquets, the poor soul himself but a wreath of old bones and falling flesh.

He stayed on the beach for an hour more, watching the seawater turn an ever-deeper blue colour. So clear was it that he could see not only the pebbles lying on the seabed, but also the ones that, years ago, had once occupied the same place before being moved on by the current. Now the wind blew harder than before, but it still barely touched the surface: like a wood plane making its first passes over a bare white log.

He got up and dusted himself down. He had fallen asleep underneath an olive tree. A red ant was crawling steadily up his left arm until he crushed it under his hand in a fit of squeamishness. The tree was squat and low and he reached up, half on his tiptoes, and picked a small, slightly pointed, unripe olive.

How old is this olive tree? he wondered. It could be more than a century old! How the ages of some trees laugh in the faces of men: seven, ten or even more generations might have passed from the moment the person first buried the seed from which the roots of this tree sprouted until the moment I picked this green olive.

The drooping trunk and branches were signs of a long, weary lifetime living out in the wind. The man recalled — the image still tender in his memory, still alive — the image of the cross, and at once had the feeling that the tree was turning into a mirror of the subject of his dream.

The still-green olive flickers like an eye,
still green enough to watch over the dead.

Alone evermore, it lacks the fortune
to chaperon the others to the press.

(The olive, the eye that observes the dead,
ripens in some corner of the garden.)

Some passer-by with idle hands selects
this olive, picking it without warning.

It will not hear the hustle or bustle
of its companions inside the mill.

But nor will it be dead –ground up and soaked
within the green oil, its heart there melting.

It had become late. He had been walking for so long, in fact, that autumn had arrived. He felt the skin twitch around and infront of his eyes and he stopped suddenly in his tracks. What really goes on under the barks of those oaks I'm headed towards? he asked himself. If only for an open wound on one of the trunks, I could thrust my fingers up through the outer flesh and into its woody centre to discern what kind of gum-like, bony dampness or resistance lies within.

The vineyard to his left had been harvested some weeks before and all of the leaves were rough corrugated and bone dry. Some were like hands that seemed to have grown old wanting to hold on to their golden treasure, their grapes, for too long, grasping only empty air in the process. Some were already on the ground and the Wanderer, a day-dreamer by nature, pictured their leafy fingers groping at the soil, trying earnestly to get closer to the spirit of the harvest that had been kickstarted months before by the verdant shoots on the vines (hands that prepare the earth only to fall into it). In September, the smell of grape juice had run free through the vineyards and along the paths, across the harvesters' skin and over the metal scissors they had clacked open and shut so many thousands of times. But by the time the Wanderer came through, the aromas had disappeared. Nor will the earth offer up any aromas until they turn over or plough it, he thought. Not until they unearth the worms and fragrant roots.

At times, the soul needs to feel the gash of the plough so that the heart can awaken from its slumber in its chest cavity.

The Wanderer pondered: there are some people whose hearts are as silent and invisible as bulbs. A bulb that doesn't germinate, whose throbbing beat is so weak it represents barely the spirit of a tremble. There are others, however, whose hearts are as visible and vibrant as the branches on a tree. A wide-open canopy in which every slender branch of blood can easily resist the song of the bird that nests in it.

An hour later on the path and he smelt the scent of burning wood. Having smelled only emptiness for the last few hours, he embraced its delicate perfume as it brought him closer to his own personal, more ancient things. He looked for the smoke but saw nothing. A pair of white flakes suddenly landed on his clothes. Had they been formed in some not too distant snow cloud they would have melted away into water on impact. But the flakes were of ash. He touched them and picked up the familiar odour on the ends of his fingers. His mind drifted back to when he would fall sleep in front of the fire as a child. He pictured himself singing gently in his bed as he listened to the sound the iron hearth brush and poker made as some family member cleaned out the grey clods of ashen cinders from the cool fireplace.

The Wanderer hadn't yet reached the oak forest but he now found himself in the sight of an old farmhouse and shed with a rude cement roof that was used to store tractors and other farming tools. The closer the man got to the house, the more intense were the guard dog's expressions of fury as it ran around the perimeter of the house behind a protective fence. As an intimidatory welcome message, quite apart from the growls and barks, the animal flashed the Wanderer its magnificently slick teeth, shiny like a set of new knives.

The man never looks the dogs that he comes across on his path in the eye, regardless of whether they're untethered and running around the pathways and trails or acting as captors in the guard of some farmhouse. That young, boistrous pup must have been his owner's best friend, serving him with proven efficiency but exacting excessive cruelty on all visitors in and around the compound. He knew the dog from before and it had always meted out the same hateful treatment. When he was in front of the dog, just a few metres away and separated only by a wire fence, the man knelt down and picked a flower to give to it as a peace offering. The barking beast, however, must have thought that the man was picking up some stone to throw at its head, hoping to silence it once and for all. Such was the racket produced by the dog that a hypothetical stone — a punishment that, of course, never came about — would have surely hit its mark, the dog's snout being scandalously oversized, enormous, almost elephantine. This was the Wanderer's final conclusion. He was able to relate abstract things in the world, inferring unpredictable consequences to the given premises.

So, with the flower still in his hand — a marigold —, and with nothing else to do with it, he left it hanging on the wire fence, snapping the slender stalk and angling it downwards so that it wouldn't drop to the ground. He had the prudence to make the break next to the corolla, where the stem was strongest. The marigold swung from one of the wire rhombi for a few seconds before the dog devoured it in the same way that most of us (and most dogs, as it happens) unconsciously devour, swallow and shut away our own personal panic. Perhaps it was the alarm, anxiety or embarrassment of never having rebelled against the tyranny of his owner, of never having known how to smash, destroy or break out of the rules of his own domesticity.

It was a marigold.
Yet in that dog's clutches
it plays but a
sad, lacerated rôle.
Between a picked flower
and one offered to bite,
there's man, dog and
the nothingness of life.

On that November night the Wanderer decided to sleep out in the open. The country didn't generally suffer from frosts at that time of year. If they were to happen, January or February were the more common months. The earth at that time still seemed to be burned out and dry from the long summer that had come before.

In order to sleep comfortably, he dug out handfuls of soil between two rows of vines and made a vaguely human-shaped relief in the dirt. Many years ago, he had visited an anthropo-morphic cemetery in which the tombs, carved out of great slabs of rock, had been decorated with the silhouettes of mostly short, childlike human bodies. The tombs were carved deep enough into the rock so that the corpses were held tightly in place on all sides.

The man scooped the soil out with his hands. Fortunately for him the earth was still quite soft, unploughed and un-worked. After a while, he had produced a deepish crater in which, despite his length, he would comfortably fit. Next, he started to excavate the place where his left arm would go, but he quickly got too tired to continue. He would sleep with his arms folded across his chest, like a corpse in his coffin.

From his haversack that he carried across his shoulder he produced a piece of splendidly mouldy blue cheese from a wrap of wax paper, and a little bit of bread. The bread crunched sharply between his famished teeth and the cheese melted on his tongue like butter.

'Ah, if only I had a bottle of wine,' he said. 'What pleasure. And then a coffee, and perhaps even a cigarette.' After his supper, he lay down in the hole, folding the arms of his corduroy anorak behind his back to use as a blanket.

It wasn't too cold. The sky was clear, and the stars were lit up like dispersed campfire embers.

His mind drifted and he thought back to the pomegranate. '*That pomegranate*,' he repeated over and over as if someone were listening. But in the midst of the dark vineyard he was all alone, snug in the soil and waiting to fall asleep. He heard the rustle of undergrowth in the distance but didn't dare raise his head from the makeshift tomb for fear of being discovered by some savage animal.

The source of the rustling was a fox with what appeared, in the darkness, to be a malformed snout. Malformed though it was, it was no tumour but rather a single swollen fruit that the beast held gently in its mouth as it wandered over to the sleeping man before leaving it on his chest. The very same pomegranate that the man had discovered and dusted off earlier in the day was now leaking juice out onto his anorak. It was a ulcerated pomegranate, the fruit of a wound that the man didn't yet know how to interpret. And as such both of them, the fruit and the man, spent a night of desolate natural death together in their makeshift tomb.

> Still life: a now open pomegranate.
> And one who sleeps, pretending he is dead.
> Tomorrow the light, at his waking hour,
> will discover death in the sleeping
> man, death that he himself won't recognise.
> Within his ancient desire to wander
> exists the thought that he who moves not, waits
> –waits for death
>   to grip him hard by the hand.

When he woke, there was no sign of the broken fruit on his chest. Nor was there, in his mind, even the most imprecise, thread-bare memory of what he had dreamt of the night before. The light, while not yet absolute, had swept away the sparks of the stars, leaving only the flare of the moon, like a piece of wine-soaked cotton wool, still illuminating the dawn mist.

He hears the rush of water but he can't know from where it comes. It is his first time on this path and he has probably crossed county lines without realising. After the forest of oaks, he has left the main path so as to discover new nooks, crannies and shades of light across the landscape. He has followed a trail that has opened up into a clearing in the midst of tall, green trees: most likely ash. Having maintained a good pace for around an hour, he now hears the gurgle of water, but its source remains hidden.

He is thirsty and wants to freshen up. Water hasn't touched his skin and he hasn't been able to wash the sleep out of his eyes since he woke in the clear light of the vineyard. He has forced the sleep out using his fingers, scraping hard into the depths of his tear ducts and noting a larger amount of soft residue than usual, as if he had been crying in one of his dreams in the night.

And still the running water is nearby, close to him, but he doesn't know where.

What if the noise is nothing more than an illusion with which to fill my hands and quench my thirst? What if its music is but imagined, not real at all? (Last night's cheese has made me very thirsty, he thinks.)

Still, he ponders. What if one day I don't clean out the sleep from my eyes? Might it form a thick crust of teardrops and send me blind? I need to find the place with water.

The *place* with water?

He climbs a small hill. A place with water would be a gorge or pond. There where the water is calm. But if water runs, it is no longer a place — it is the passage of time.

It now starts to rain.

Rainwater is neither a place nor the passage of time. The vertical nature of its flow is nothing more than a ghostly fantasy.

Trampled rainwater cannot quench a man's thirst. Just as crushed teardrops cannot quench a heart's pain: it more often than not enrages it. To cry from pain — now the Wanderer has a vague sense of dreaming about something the night before, something that he not yet knows — is to dress a wound without treating it.

Finally, he found the water. It was a small spring from which water gushed and bubbled. The man was so thirsty that he didn't bother to put his hands under the water but rather laid out on his back and placed the nape of his neck on the green wreathed stony semi-circle.

The spurt of water went straight into the Wanderer's mouth, as if rooting itself deep in his body. Lying prone next to the spring, his body and soul given over to the gushing stream, he watched the lush beech tree at the edge of the opening as it seemed to grow up, over and across the humble niche, suckling on it like a new born baby does its wet nurse.

He has made a cup with his gaping mouth,
and not with his hands. The man now drinking,
now truly does so with his whole form: his
bones, his flesh, heart, blood and skin. He lies down
at the foot of that spring, soaking himself
–the mouth where the stream grows makes a basin.
He seems not now the avid Wanderer:
the stream from the beech tree nourishes him.

He walked for a long time and went to rest in a steep-pitched field. At its top end there seemed to him to be a hut built of dark rocks and so he determined to reach it before nightfall, huffing and puffing as he went up the steep slope. There was not a soul in the field. Well, there must have been — despite being buried — the souls of cows, sheep and rams, foxes and wolves. Because animals, too, must have souls. Even if nobody remembers them.

He reached the hut after around an hour of walking. It had a shoddy wooden door that didn't close properly, and the roof was half caved in. For dinner, he ate three apples that he had plucked from an apple tree in an orchard. They were not yet fully ripe but were juicy and sweet to taste. He was hungry and scoured the cores of all three before licking greedily at the pips.

Exhausted and covered in scratches from having spent the whole day traipsing along innumerable paths, he would sleep inside the hut. Wouldn't it be terrible, he thought, if a bad wind blew up and knocked over the stones, leaving me here, crushed and helpless?

He thought this. 'How very silly,' he said to himself. But the thought, whilst perhaps a little wild, wasn't *that* silly. His body adapted to the shape of the ground, the grass and the mud under the tumult of stones while his spirit watched out over the valley like a dark, noble warden in the funerary monument to the unknown Wanderer.

He lay down on the grass with his empty knapsack folded up as a cushion. He hadn't spoken to anyone for days. The night was dark and the moon had just started to wax. The Wanderer rolled over to his left-hand side and immediately got up in shock. What brightness is that? Is my weariness making me see things?

But no. When he brought his face closer to the sparks, kneeling down onto the ground, he saw the source of the light: it was a great collection of fireflies. There were a great many, all seemingly competing to see which could shine the brightest. When he woke up a few hours later, he thought nothing of it: another night and another dream he was unable to interpret.

> All of them were burning, a blaze shining white:
> there were more than twenty fireflies glowing bright.
> They all died slowly out, and a moribund
> yellow brightness was left still encircling
> each tinder of each body. Shadows within,
> all the fireflies were but worms of dry grass.

The next day he crossed over to the other side of the mountain. He came from loose black layers of shorn slate that periodically cut through the land, open fields full of cereals and occasional trees. On the new side of the mountain, however, the trees wrestled and jostled with each other for canopy space and aromas of mushrooms and fermenting matter pervaded everything. Light shone across countless objects and infinite rocks. The place was darker, more shaded, and the man felt it in the cold on his bare neck. It felt as if autumn had finished and winter had begun.

> If he could but exchange the season as
> easily as the passenger changes

trains! In but a flash the summer heat gives
way to the February frozen wastes!

As he had, from the very first day, wandered aimlessly, he
started to descend the slope until he saw in the distance a few
houses that must have made up part of some long-forgotten
hamlet. Before reaching the village, however, the man came
across a small cemetery. The iron gate was ajar with no latch or
chain to stop people from pushing it open and going inside. *Et
Lux Perpetua Luceat Eis* had been inscribed above the gateway.
Below it, *Any 1896* had been carved in Catalan.

He pushed open the gate and walked on through, preparing
himself to recieve homage from all the unknown bodies. A
tabby cat that was walking amongst the tombs and crosses
noticed him and stopped to stare for a few seconds. Its gaze,
bright and piercing; its steps, shrewd.

A cat with a glimmering gaze
walks among gravestones and crosses.
Those once living are now condemned
to the shadows and grassy earth.

Wreaths of flowers fall here and there,
unburied upon the tombstones.
The Wanderer ponders: how quick
the body's hours do elapse!

The cat asks itself: and the soul?
Of these folk, is anything left,
but a handful of memories?

The man: in death are we the same?
The lover, honest or cruel,
oft lingering in his absence?

Leaving the cemetery, he headed towards the hamlet that he had seen from afar. It was a loose collection of ancient, unpainted stone houses with sloped roofs. Each house had its own chimney, but at that moment smoke only rose from one of them.

'The last house in the village is as lonely and isolated as the last house at the edge of the world,' whispered the Wanderer, remembering verses by a poet from Prague. It was the last house in the village, true, but for him, coming from an unknown path not yet incumbered by tarmac or cement, it also represented the very first.

It's the ultimate house of the hamlet,
that which the Wanderer had passed first by
–but the house itself had, perhaps, found him.
Where is it? Segarra or Judea?

The man spies the manure steam out the back.
There are white sheets hanging up out the front.
His journey's fate does carry him along:
it's the sole thing that respires in the fumes.

Behind the window there perches a cage.
The goldfinch inside forthwith strikes up a
sombre song. That which utters not a word

is the calm, docile puppy made of clay,

modelled and made and painted by a child,
sitting in the centre of the table.
And to complete the ring of the fable,
a calendar marked by a reindeer sketch.

And even if a pan boiled over flame,
even if the radio still sounded,
even if he'd seen washing still hanging,
he would still have known he'd got to *Nowhere*.

He knocks at the door but nobody answers. It is unlocked
so he pushes it open and walks inside. 'Good morning,' he says
in a loud, clear voice. He waits for a while. Perhaps this is a
farmhands' house and they have gone out to graze the herd.
He casts an eye around the kitchen and opens one or two of
the drawers. All the knives are scratched, and the spoons are
stained red with rust around the upper part that touches the
tongue and teeth. In one of the two bedrooms, he is surprised
by the bare carcass of a towering double bed frame made from
dark, coffee-coloured wood. Only the frame remains: there
is no mattress. The room smells musty, as if the air has spent
many years trapped in there, kidnapped, without any chance
of escape. The mirror that presides over the bedroom is set
into an ancient frame on which dance four or five long-locked
nymphs. Two of these water nymphs' hair, sculpted out of rus-
tic plaster, run around the mirror from right to left, knotting
together into one at the bottom as if the girls were about to
jump off the frame together and into a gorge, linked not by

their hands, but by their flowing locks. In the greying, oxidised mirror, the Wanderer sees himself as significantly older than he is. When he discovers that his eyebrows have merged together to form a dark, hairy stain above his disconcerted gaze, he quickly decides to leave the house and return to his path.

The Wanderer has fled the abandoned house, but has not yet shaken off the feeling of a family's presence.

There is nobody else in the rest of the village. When he passes under the open window of another house, he hears the tap of a fork against a plate: someone, now long gone, is making an omelette. A little further away, he finds a fountain with a rounded, shell-shaped tap. A burst of sandy water springs forth as he turns it. Where does the sand come from if the nearest beach is more than fifteen days away as the crow flies? Once the stream of water has run dry, he turns the tap again and more sand is dislodged before clean water starts to bubble out, further dispersing the brown grains within. Before draining away, he briefly — a matter of seconds — sees his reflection in the water that lingers in the black stone dish. To his relief, it is no longer the face that appeared to him in the mirror.

Still, the man broods on his experience in the house. He can't understand the smoking chimney and the empty fireplace: there were no ashes, no firewood. The alcove, too, where somebody had left a wooden box full of tools. The fireplace chains hanging as if from a drawbridge. He remembers the woodworm holes in the enormous wooden bed. There were so many!

The deceased spirits, while they were sleeping,
had sneaked in through the woodworms' corridors.
Finding wormwood food is hard work indeed!
Unaware, the sleeping ones passed away,
wandering off path, between the crossroads.
(The fire of the deceased burnt the mattress.)

On the road out of the village he hears again the tap of the fork against the bowl and he remembers that, many years ago, he had written some lines of poetry about just that pretext, a poem that now seems to him to have predicted his time in this empty village — a *haunted village*, perhaps —, this dead village where the only living soul is a shabby tabby cat.

He tries to coax the old poem from his memory and, at first, the verses resist (he had been reminded of the poem by the tap-tap of a fork against a bowl against the silence of the street). Back on his path the frozen verses have slowly melted and come back to him, but being rhyming verses of a couple of stanzas, he has found it more difficult than usual. If he hadn't visited the village, he would probably never have been able to recall them. It's as if the text itself had anticipated the experience. At times, art doesn't imitate life, but rather, in advance, carves out its experiences as it sees fit:

It is a cold, grey, wet day. A winter
Sunday at first light. All of the paths are
deserted and, likewise, so are the squares.

Only a bell tower shows signs of life,
a humble bell set into the belfry:
it rings always in time, prompting us all.

The neighbour sleeps: the vengeance of his work.
Abandoned wreaths lie on the balconies.
Suddenly there sounds the clinking of mugs,
dishes and cutlery. Hunger awakes.
No one need go to the forest to dine.
As such, who beats the eggs for the omelette?

The Wanderer never stopped. He ate whatever he found along his way (fruits, leaf vegetables, cuts of meat that might have caught his eye in some market but that he now scavenged from under the watchful interest of groups of sticky flies, bread of dubious quality). He slept wherever he could (open fields, abandoned haystacks and caves). He was truly a wanderer, the sole protagonist of a journey that defied both time and space.

He started to teach himself how to read and interpret the sky. He learnt tell whether or not the clouds or fog banks that sat on the peaks of a distant mountain range carried rain in them or not. He particularly liked to read the negative imprint of the daytime sky: he learnt the names of the constellations and the positions of the orbiting bodies, shining like stones lying in a field, that coursed the heavens at night. At times, from one night to another, he lost sight of certain stars, causing him great anguish. Such was his memory of them that it felt as if someone had ripped them off and away from him and the night's black page, treacherously uprooting them in the darkness.

It was one of those evenings when the Wanderer found himself searching for a place to sleep. Fairly confident that a convenient spot wasn't too far away, he was soon distracted by the beautiful bright lights in the early night sky and it was just when he was looking up and lost in the nocturnal black that he bumped into that woman who, like him, was walking the star-lit paths on foot. She was wearing a blue patchwork dress and was not particularly beautiful, but had a deeply attractive, almost enchanting gaze. Her generally well proportioned figure was on the short and thin side. What stood out about her, however, were the enormous, round veins on her hands (not even the Saint Peter in my local church has veins like those, thought the man). Surely, if you looked at them for too long, they'd scare you half to death. She must have been a farmworker and used to heavy loads, but at that moment the woman carried nothing but her blue dress and bulging veins: no coarse sack, no basket, no crops.

The woman had stopped on the path for a moment and had been staring at the ground as if looking for worms or some fleeting fire sprite's footprints and the man didn't see her until it was too late. He apologised profusely to the apparently shocked woman. Of course, if a man rudely crashes into a woman on a lonely path away from the outlying houses of the village, the first thing that one suspects is not that the man was distracted while looking up at the luminous composition of the firmament. He quickly apologised again and explained the reason behind his momentary clumsiness. The woman, having also spent many years staring up at the night-time skies, seemed to understand immediately. She replied that the best time to view the sky was at the break of dawn, when the stars were the brightest. Well, so compelling did she find the star-struck man, wandering aimlessly on that dark path, that after a while she grew quite fond of him and so invited him back to her house for a glass of milk.

The house was simple and cosy and there was a large, unvarnished wooden table standing in the small dining room. At the centre of the table, instead of a vase or bowl of apples or lemons, there were two crossed knitting needles and a half-finished pile of something that seemed destined to become a claret-red pullover. The unfinished shape of what the woman had so far knitted reminded the man of the disjointed starry constellations that he had been staring at just before meeting her — if but she had had time to bring all the bright points into one line.

The woman took two glasses out of one of the kitchen cupboards and filled them to the brim with milk that she poured from a firm-handled tin pitcher. The lid on the spout bobbed gently with the flow of the liquid and the milk in the glasses frothed and bubbled before calming and settling for the man and woman to bring the glasses up to their lips and drink. The man pictured a fountain of milk flowing through his host's hands and he wondered if her breasts had ever spilled forth into a baby's mouth. But he didn't dare to ask. They drank and moved their glasses together without touching, holding each other's gaze. 'Cheers!' said the man.

The Wanderer was walking, distracted.
He knows not where he goes. Nor she from where

he comes. They wait to drink a glass of milk.
She knows not from where that strange man comes, he
knows still less of her, and that of her life.
He hardly knows from where it had come, his
desire or delirium to escape.
To focus his eyes, to stay ever mute?
To exist no more in his own shadow,
tied not to the rudder of that old ship,
carried down to the sea by the river?
Somebody has just materialised
with whom the man can share a glass of milk.
Someone, unlike him, lost in deepest thought.
The Milky Way has brought them together.

From the window in the woman's bedroom, the Wanderer watched a stork in flight. It flapped its wings powerfully, as if shaking out a table cloth, and quickly drifted across a tenuous, early morning sky that was changing white to blue. The man could tell he was far from home because there were no storks where he was from and so there were none of the enormous nests they build on church spires or pylon platforms.

The woman wasn't there. She must have got up early to go to work outside. From the bed where he was lying, the Wanderer heard the whinnying of horses.

He felt as light as the stork; the vastness of the sky held no limits for him. Here, on earth, where everything is very different, one is constantly pushing up against a border of some sort: a cliff face, a wall, a river, borders. He thought for a while longer before leaning out of the window to try to follow the stork's trajectory, but it had already faded away into the nothingness. He was about to call out to the woman, but realised that he didn't know her name. He could have invented a name — Aurora, Celeste —, if only to feel close to her again. But no, he stayed quiet. Turning away from the window, he looked down at the unfamiliar, unrecognisable, unmade bed and it reminded him of one of those poor, empty villages, bereft of all life.

He thought of the stork and of the vigorous urge that had come over him just moments before to be something completely alien to what he was before and his deep desire to finally unburden himself, not just from his own conscience, but from conscience in its entirety. But in truth, now that he thought about it, he was not inclined to be the bird that, flashing by the window frame, was most likely looking for food for its offspring — or was perhaps already carrying it back to them in the voids of its beak. The stork was not free: it had to follow its instinct so as to fulfil that which was prescribed in its being. Its destiny had already been written. The man, on the other hand, was now starting to feel free to do what he wanted to do; if necessary, to choose, even, his own means and moment of death. To reinforce more than ever what he was (or what he wanted to be) and, if required, to reject both things in full.

> He wants not to be a
> stork, or a soaring hawk.
> Or to rummage remains
> with a vulture's brusque beak.

Wants not to be a bird:
no eagle or skylark.
Be a man, live in peace:
he wants for nothing more.

He wants not to be a
starling or a red breast.
He, himself, is no bird:

nor, yet, a nightingale!
He wants only to feel
the joy of being free.

He went outside to look for the woman who had taken him in for the night. Circling round the house, he saw a small patch of abandoned land that was overgrown with weeds and filled with rubble. In amongst the crumbled fragments of broken bricks and tiles, there gleamed the colour and decorative borders of an old mosaic.

Again, he felt the urge to call out to her; he didn't feel comfortable waking up in the bed of an unknown woman with whom he had spent but some waking hours the night before, only to now be the sole lord and master of her home. Just at that moment, however, he heard the sound of footsteps accompanied by the woman's voice in conversation with someone else. The man couldn't make out the whole conversation, but it soon became clear that his host was talking about him in less than promising terms: 'wanted… touch anything… yesterday… nothing else but… today… time to milk… and coming back… dead.' As her voice drew closer the guest realised that the woman had gone to get help from the other person who, judging by the grunts that he made, seemed to be male. When the two of them finally entered the house, the Wanderer was able to follow the whole conversation from his hiding place. He then well understood why the woman had lied as she insisted once again as to the reason why she must have gone out to look for help:

'This is why I offered him my bed. But when I knocked on the door this morning there was no answer. I knocked again, and still nothing. So, I opened the door and I went up to him and HE WAS AS STIFF AS A FROZEN BRANCH! So cool was his skin that it sent shivers down my spine. Oh! What do you think we should do?'

Why do these people think that I am dead?

He dashed out of the house as fast as he could. Perhaps they are the ones who are dead, he thought. Dead like everything else in the last few hours has been dead: the woman and her friend; the whinnying horses; the stork that appeared in an instant against the blue backdrop of the window; even the woman and her one-night stand? Perhaps he was the only one there who could give testimony to so much death (and perhaps so little memory).

Why do they think me dead?
Why do they all think that?
I've not fallen of late,
I feel happy and strong,
a person full and whole,
no piece of mosaic!

What if it is they who
are dead? Ever sickly
on the callow pages,
obituary tales,
escaping in their death,
desiring not to grow
used to eyes or concerns;
as if, naïvely, it
might rescue me from time,
granting eternal life,
seeing it as milk, not
pus; no wound but a gift.

The Pomegranate Tree moves on. But have you asked yourselves who this man is, this character we call the *Wanderer*, the main character of the unusual journey set out in none other than this poem?

Have you noticed the pointed, almost knife-like contours of his face? Ah, of course not; I have not yet described his appearance. An eagle-like nose, skinny ears with pointed lobes, thin lips and sharp cheekbones as if sculpted with a gouge from the heart of some trunk — or with a chisel from a block of marble — producing and planting, in one foul swoop, this man's face into his body.

On the walker's body, all is pointed:
the absence of a wife made him this way.
They were once two heads on the same pillow.

The woman, one day, like someone jotting
down some item she needed to buy, took
a scrap of paper and stuck it on the fridge.
It said: *I'm not coming back.* Still, the man
waits ever less, without any complaint.
The loss of his wife has made him this way.
The first few months turned his spirit −with the
increasing dark pain that slowly undid
his heart, too− into a pointed shadow.

As wounded wolves howl, caught between the steel teeth
of a snare, waiting for the wound to heal or their lives to bleed
out, so did the man cry in the first few days after his wife
had left. He never again ate apple pie and refused to listen to
piano music. If he found himself reading or writing in a bar
and a *Nocturne* by Chopin or some improvised piece by Keith
Jarrett resonated across the room, the Wanderer — before he
wandered — would pay the bill and leave.

Throughout those long days and months, he felt the absence
of his wife like a morose haemorrhage, slowly dripping and
painful. There is little love in this word, *haemorrhage.*

After that, the man — who, until then, had never showed
any interest in walking — started to leave his flat more
and more frequently. It suffocated him. He burned all of her
things: two silk scarves that she had left on her bedside table;
various books; five or six words or expressions — compass,
relapse, moderately, *ergo* and parched — that the woman often

used; an engraving that he had given to her a couple of years before; a piece of wood she used to measure out quantities of spaghetti. One day, walking aimlessly around the city, the man passed in front of a house that was being built. He smelt, first of all, plaster that reminded him of other houses he had seen under construction, perhaps even taking him back to the flat where he lived as a small child, that which he had visited with his parents when it was nothing more than an empty shell of freshly plastered walls and rough floors of tiled meshing waiting to be waxed over. He also smelt the perfumed aroma of wood as it hung in the air. Well, it is quite possible that the smell wasn't coming from the house under construction, but rather from the neighbouring one that was being refurbished and into which some workmen were hauling furniture. But the woody fragrance did not come from the pre-made, neatly delivered furniture itself. No, it was such an intense, fresh woody aroma that a carpenter must have been somewhere inside working away with his plane or, more likely, his saw. It was the smell of freshly injured wood: the shavings landing on the floor must have still been hot from the tools.

The two smells — the wood and the plaster — were a clear sign of things to come: he would never build a house himself. Perhaps some day, though, he might just own one. He would leave the very next day without knowing where he was going. On one of the first days on his rudder-less path, just after his experience with the pomegranate, he entered a forest of black pines. It was there where he thought back to the aromas — the plaster, the wood — he had smelt emanating from the suburban houses under construction or being restored. It had rained in the forest that day and the pine needles were running quick with green water. Despite it being a wild space, open to all animals, the smells of the forest that day were as hospitable and welcoming as that of the wood and plaster.

If you lose yourself in the woods,
be patient, walker, don't despair.
Look to meet and see the fleeting
presence of a wandering soul.

And listen well to what he tells
you, his sad, sad story of woe.
'Restore your heart, place it in the
space of the now,' says the singer.

Fear not the savage fauna, the
scorpion under stone. Rather,
think of the ancient oak and holm,
have faith in the pine and cedar.

As all make for good company,
dark though it is, melancholy!

The melancholia which the Wanderer suffered from was dark indeed. It led him to follow his desultory path for weeks on end. Yet every day that passed and every new adventure made him feel a little better. He looked at things differently. He saw a telegraph pole by the side of the road and imagined the rustling vibrations within the dead wood. Do the trees used in wooden ships echo with the rough sound of the seabed, a place where they would sooner drop roots and grow than lay anchor? He remembered the poem by that Irish poet about the rain-stick, those tubes filled with a handful of imprisoned grains that, when turned upside down, create the music of falling rain. As if we were gods capable of capturing the liquefaction of the clouds.

Just at that moment he heard the sudden deafening bang of electricity cables, until then hanging dead like rope in a well, jumping into life in the evening light, running and burning like dominoes with an infinity of furious sparks. The Wanderer assumed that all of the wires had been feeding off the light of some mysterious well — the well at the edge of life —, and that the light was now running down towards the earth.

He turned and quickly ran over to where a boy was lying dead on the ground next to his motorcycle. The boy was flat on his back with his helmet pointing upwards around ten metres away from the telegraph pole that he had crashed into. The collision had been so severe that, in spite of the protection afforded by his helmet, the boy had died instantly. All of his internal organs had come undone. The Wanderer then understood where the light, smashed into thousands of consecutive sparks, far from where the Wanderer was standing next to the boy's carcass, had gone. It had disappeared faster than the poor boy's soul.

Walking, ever walking, he reached a point on his path that looked down over a group of new houses. Just before reaching the shadow of a local stone cross that stood by the side of the road (that in the midday light looked more like an archer with his bow than a cross), he heard a siren wail. It reminded him of a factory and of the dirty faced workers downing their tools and leaving *en masse* in their filthy boiler suits before crossing paths with other, fresher faced workers with cleaner attire, their lunchtime sandwiches still neatly wrapped up under their arms. But the village below seemed too small to have a factory close by. All the houses were of the same height and there were no giant chimneys filling the sky with waste. In front of him, instead, was a green river that wound its way down through a canyon. He realised that the sound had followed the same watercourse, using the orography of the terrain as a loud speaker so as to be heard far and wide, a long way from its place of creation.

But who was the siren calling, and why?

He continued along his path. There was a pig farm around two hundred metres away from him on the outskirts of the village and he had picked up the stench of the stabled beasts long before seeing the building's run-down architecture and bare brick walls. Once in front of the building and making sure nobody could see him, he stood on his tiptoes and reached up, grabbed the top of the open wall (there was around a metre between the top of the wall and the roof) and pulled himself up to take a quick look inside. (Someone had written what was most probably the owner's name and telephone number on the wall in dripping black paint). Inside were six pigs in a space of no more than ten square metres and the floor was covered with a foul mixture of mud, straw, excrement and the occasional dead mouse. The door was made of metal and sported two large bolts. He pulled himself further up so that he was able to put one leg over the wall and straddle it. Without really thinking what he was doing, he jumped down into the pen. The pigs snorted nervously but didn't bother him, rather moving away as if dubious of his intentions. The man then slid the two bolts across the door and, pushing hard on the loins of one of the pigs, guided it through the gap and out into the open. With the animal outside, he bolted the door closed again and climbed back up and over the wall. The rolling midday sun shone down on the poor pink beast, naked and miserable, not knowing what to do. It oinked and rustled its snout in amongst some grasses.

A pig escapes the sty,
as the court of a pig
is named (don't be foolish:
think not of the court of
a king. A pig is clean
at heart. The king, not so).
Nor is the pig the king
of the hamlet. The whole
world watches monarchs as
they live off the effort
of others, filling their
coffers. If we compare
hearts, the sow's does frighten,
so large and blue in death.
Small like a red berry,
and guilded by fortune,
the king's glimmering heart,
a brightly shining star.
Helpful soul by nature,
the pig senses the blade
long before the butcher
opens his stream of blood.

No thurible exists
that would reduce the mud
of his vile life and times.
If kings are kings, it is
due only to the numb
nature of the first of
our species who let them.
From that moment onwards,
kings and queens have aimed to
maintain the *status quo*,
this way of living, king
o'er distracted subjects.
Laws are in their favour,
they ignore the ballots
and their votes, their people
do make them laugh out loud.
And, like a drop of wine,
they swallow back the lies
that the person blessed with
the sacred crown invents.
They accept such insults
as they are only men.
They should, however, know
that no king has blue blood.
Red and flowing freely,
when stuck by some sharp thing,
still if it's made of gold,
or when receiving the
embrace —and dying, then—
of the tip of a knife.

The old man looked like a shepherd without his flock. 'You shouldn't have done that,' he said. He was followed by a dog that had probably once been a sheep-dog, but that was by then also flock-less. The man was around sixty or seventy years old and looked like a thin, rigid bean-pole. When he turned his neck, his bones made a sound like creaky old door hinges. The dog had three or four ticks under his ears. It scratched at its neck violently as it rubbed itself up against the rough stones and plants at the side of the path until the old man gave it a whack. This despite the fact that the dog's neck didn't make nearly as terrible a noise as his own. 'Idiot!' he shouted angrily. 'You'll leave the spur in!'

'What shouldn't I have done?' asked the Wanderer.

'You let that pig out,' replied the man.

He didn't understand. The flock-less shepherd had come from the opposite direction. It was impossible for him to know about what had happened less than an hour before.

'The animal got scared and ran about for a while before, not knowing the terrain, it fell down from the Timba de l'Albat,' said the shepherd.[1] 'More than two hundred kilos of meat, now not good for nothing but for fattening up the vultures that fly around looking for scraps at the bottom.'

(They called it — and for good reason — the Timba de l'Albat because years before a pregnant woman had slipped and fallen there. They found her on her back at the bottom of the gorge. She died, but they were able to save the baby after two months of intensive hospital care. The child lived for four more years before it, too, died of diphtheria. Nobody can remember

[1]   *Timba de l'Albat* translates as The Child's Precipice

whether the name 'Albat' refers to the day of the fatal fall or the day, four years later, when the child passed away. Either way, if city streets and avenues can be named after invading generals who once inflicted violence and misery on the same places that now bear their names, why should we worry ourselves about the name of some precipice in some remote village?).

'Let which pig out?' replied the Wanderer. 'How do you know that I...? And how has news of the pig's fate travelled so fast? Not even *I* was aware of it!'

Was this a warning? Was this a sign? What if the pig, knowing that its end was near, had chosen that much nobler death instead of accepting its destiny like its companions?

> From time to time, a piece of news stands out
> to make us aware that nothing is free.
> One must, knowing this, show one's gratitude:
> it will help you smash open the surface
>   of your '*self*' that is so often constrained.
> You're very aware of that day you fell,
> a hardened heart hoping for new terrain
> –soil not yet destroyed by good common sense.

He continued to wander unknown pathways, often thinking about the pig and its untimely death. Fear and the foreign setting had led the animal to jump into the abyss. But what if the pig had brought about its demise on purpose? It is supposed that an animal's instinct is to survive, to run away from annihilation. But what do we know about a pig's instincts? Have we ever been inside one of these animals' heads? And what's more, how can we know if they are all cut from the same cloth or not?

He imagined it tumbling down the bluff until something — a solid tree trunk or stubborn rock — stopped it, its body broken, its gaze shocked still. An animal that had always been kept locked up, shut up in a tiny space, then in free-fall. The effort of the run to the gorge was repaid by the excitement of flying through the air before ceasing to be: that body, now a dead weight, airborne, without *terra firma* under its trotters, was, at that moment, more alive than it had ever been. It didn't begrudge the man having opened the gate to the pigsty. Far from it. The weather was turning cold. What day was it? What was the time? Which month? It must have been autumn. How many days had he been walking? Twenty, thirty? That pig, he thought, had anticipated its own death by three months. As if it had pictured the bench on which it would have been tortured, felt the force with which they would have held down its limbs so that it couldn't kick out, felt the slice of the cold cut into its meaty neck, stretched out in hot blood. As if it had already seen the steam rising up out of its open body as it was cut up and quickly salted. As if it had heard the sinister voice of the butcher singing out its body parts (loins, fillets, ribs) as he cut them out and handed them over to someone else. The pig's entire pain is used up: what little noise its innards make upon the table! And how pure the pain boils within the metal bowls!

We know that within our frames there is blood.
We know there is even more water. The
rivers of blood, the pond shaped in our form.
And there is, much more than water and blood,

the commotion that our memories raise
up. The resistant dust of memories
slowly come together, turning to stone,
forming a pebble, a nodule of pain.
Blood and water have always been body:
nutrition, irrigation. This stone is
new. It's an obstacle: never conceived.
And, specifically: it's an illness.
One must, as doctors say, 'take care of it',
meaning nothing more than expelling it.
It is not the kidney that made the stone.
It's the heart's secret sculptor, maintaining
the piece of work safe between its fibres.
(This sculptor, in particular, prefers
the dark art of pain, intriguing to all).
It finds it difficult to escape from.
The heart, as ever, so hospitable!
(I might well have written *hospital*: the
heart is no hospital, but rather the
patient. The stone is not ill, but rather
the pain). Blood and water could dissolve it,
but they're unable to locate the stone;
biology could just melt it away,
a circular strike –bodies have many
resources. We should 'take care of' the stone,
eradicate it, unroot it from the
heart. If it poisons the blood, it means that
this stone, having amassed time with fragments
of images, memories and voices,
apart from the heart, has subdued the mind.

For so many days had he been walking that his legs were tired and, what's more, he had a fever. He wasn't yet sure what he was looking for, but he knew what he was running from and that he was very far from home.

The lush green landscape that had accompanied him on the majority of his journey had now disappeared. The land he trod was dry and there were only a few trees — poplars, he guessed — when running water was nearby. Here, without the warmth of the trees, on that vast open plain dotted with occasional derelict houses, he would be colder. But it wasn't the temperature that he worried about, it was the fatigue he felt in his muscles and bones and, more than anything, the prickly burning sensation in his temples and forehead that made his whole body feel weak.

When he was a child, his grandmother, leaning over his bed and placing her hand momentarily, reverently on his brow, would tell him that 'fever will make you grow half a centimetre.' But the Wanderer had stopped growing many years before. And many years had also passed since his grandmother had died. It was the first death to make the man cry, back when he was barely twelve years old.

Fever makes children grow,
his grandma always said.
It used to make him fume
to feel her frosty hand
on his burning forehead.
Better off alone, was
he. Doing what he liked
in that deserted house.

Fever, said his grandma,
makes children's bodies grow.
She had her tranquil eyes
within her thoughtful gaze.
Her hand would feel his brow,
a lazy, roaming stroke,
and in that caring tone,
she'd say: 'Sleep. Tomorrow
you will feel much better.'
But taller he was not.
His grandma, one morning,
never again got up.
It was his first real woe.
The boy he grew up quick.
And it wasn't due to
the fever: it was her
cry that night that guided
the woman to her grave.

He met the woman at a fork in the road. She was coming along another path and they met at the juncture where the two tracks became one. She carried a large bundle on her back that she held down tightly with a rope. Her hair was completely grey while her face was smooth, unwrinkled and untouched by the sun, as if the woman were little more than twenty-five years old. Her shawl was tatty around the edges and her shoes — very worn leather boots with laces — were painful to behold: both soles had come unstuck and yawned wide open with every step she took.

'Good morning, sir. These are fine paths to walk alone, don't you think?' The woman spoke in a strange tongue and the man wasn't sure if it was just a dialect of his own speech or another, completely different, language that was just similar enough to his own for him to be able to understand. 'I'd like to show you something, if I could just have a few minutes of your time,' continued the woman.

They walked together for a while. The fledgling-faced old woman asked him where he was headed and he replied that his walk (he called it a *walk*, even though it had transformed into something quite different many days before) was not necessarily a journey through space, but rather a journey through time.

'And so what are you running from, sir, if you don't mind me asking?'

The man thought carefully before responding.

'Running away… I'm not running away from anything or anybody in particular,' he said. 'I suppose I'm running away from that which I might have been or that which I might have ended up being if I hadn't started off on this long walk.'

'So, would you say you are looking for another *you*?' asked the woman.

'Not exactly. I started my wanderings to distance myself from the person I once was and that, slowly but surely, over long days, I had stopped being. And I don't yet know who I will become, if I will ever become someone different from who I once was.'

Here, he bit his lip and thought better of the words that he was about to say.

'I suppose I want to abandon my old disguises, so to speak.'

Just as the words had left his mouth, the Wanderer was overcome by a sudden dizziness. He sat down on a large rock that had been daubed with red and black paint. A solitary pine, the only tree that the man had seen for a long while, loomed over him. A great darkness spread out, growing everywhere, and the fading light of day no longer cast the shadows of their two bodies onto the earth.

'I think I'm ill,' said the Wanderer. The woman put her bundle on the ground and undid the tight knot that held it together. Opening her bag, an aroma of dry herbs floated up and into the air. She rummaged inside it for a moment before taking something out.

'Chew on this root for a while and you'll feel better,' she said.

He looked at it suspiciously before accepting it and putting it in his mouth. Taking a cautious bite, he spat it onto the ground like a smoker spits out a cigar end before lighting it up.

'You have to keep chewing on it so that your wisdom teeth slowly break down the dark parts of the bark. Its extract will refresh your palate and seep into your gums. It'll make you feel better, you'll see.'

The woman moved to touch her hand against the man's forehead to feel his temperature but he flinched violently away from her as if she were the devil himself.

The root didn't taste all that bad and, just as the woman had said, its juice ran out as he continued to chew on it. Earthy to touch, it was quite fresh to taste.

Exhausted, he started to nod off. The woman sat down next to him to stop him from falling over to one side and hurting himself on a rock. She put her arm around his shoulder and he rested his sleepy head on it. Perhaps he was dreaming of the *I* that he was running from, the one who had once rested his head on the same pillow that he had shared every night with that other woman, the one that he had once dared to call his own.

> The girl half embraced him.
> Who will stop us falling?
> A passing fox and the
> drawing of the plough in
> the bark of a lone pine,
> there upon the cold earth.
> The day grows older. Yes,
> the tree grows far from the
> copse. It has no warming
> support from the others,
> and has never said *we*.
> But better will it see
> itself in the mirror
> of some pond, created
> by the rain: sharp roots, parts
> of trunks still rising up,
> green, outstretched branches that
> tangle up the sun and
> all else that gets lost in
> there, left behind –happy
> days, firm proclamations
> of dedication, plans
> undone and great plots that
> come apart at the seams.

He woke up at the break of dawn, not knowing where he was or what he was doing wrapped up under the strange blanket that, when he held it up in front of his face, revealed itself to be a woman's tatty old shawl. He was laid out on a rock and remembered nothing of the night before. Nor did he feel the symptoms of the fever that had made him so weak just a few hours before. It felt as though the new day had borne them away along with a few degrees of warmth and the muddy memory of an enigmatic medicine woman.

> She no longer hugs him.
> The Wanderer knows not
> that, sleeping deeply, he
> had rested his head there.
> He has lost all sign of
> the woman from last night.

> From the *Piety* that
> the two of them once formed,
> left resting on a rock,
> the man now brought back from
> nightmares and fears, as if
> resurging from a stump.

Pain is what makes our bodies real, thought the Wanderer. This pain running through the veins in my wrist, for example, as if the tubes themselves had suddenly narrowed, causing the squeezed blood to push harder. Or like the mineral pain from my bones as they complain in their dull, constant voice.

It is also pain that makes our souls feel more palpable.

Have you ever heard of a soul that didn't suffer? Have you ever known one that wasn't scathed in some way?

The body rarely relives the symptoms of its pain. The soul, on the other hand, delights in them regularly. It's not necessary. Too much pain is dirty business. When physical pain disappears, the body tends to forget. But even when pain has disappeared from the soul or is, at least, well-worn, there is an echo that pervades in its stony cavity, the sound of a cracking. You would do well to remember this.

On the 10th of July 2012, the man we have come to know as the Wanderer received a phone call from a friend. This friend told him that the illness which he had been suffering from for more than a year had finally got the better of him and asked him if he would go and visit him at the *Hospital Clínic* in Barcelona, as he wanted to talk. After that first meeting, the two men started to meet regularly, at least twice a week.

'I have a twenty percent chance of getting through this,' said the man.

The last time the two friends saw each other was three weeks before his death on the 13th of October of the same year. The only people to see him after that were the sick man's wife and his close family.

Long before his journey, this series of events had profoundly affected the Wanderer, though he didn't realise it until later. Some experiences need a long time to digest, like snakes that consume bodies that are much larger than their own.

The sick man's surname was the same as the plant that produces pomegranates. The pomegranate is an autumn fruit.

Life is the offensive attack of fate.
And death, that which stops it from happening.
Life, how many years will you serve as home?
And you, death, eternal desert of sand!

The man, now finding himself in a barren, tree-less land, suddenly realised the meaning of the pomegranate that, some time before, had detached itself from its branch to be discovered on his path. The fruit found him, too, so that he would know which path to follow.

It is no reddish hand.
It's reddish like a heart.
It trembles, falls and dies,
that form of sickly blood.

When seed is sown in field,
it quickly, then, dries out.
Red blood: the heart demands,
naked in the ribcage.

The falling of the fruit,
the fading of the light
of the body and soul.

When the pain lingers on —
heart, be like the hotel
porter on the nightshift.

He sensed his journey was finally coming to an end. He was tired and felt that he had discovered that which he needed to continue his life. But before turning and heading back home, he decided to spend just a few more days on the road.

That morning he walked at a good pace, crossing a river over a rickety wooden bridge whose boards swayed under his feet. Once again he found himself in forests of birch and chestnut. He discovered a lake on his route northwards and saw wide open fields of clay soils. He discovered meadows where red cows pastured and black and white horses played chaotic chess matches across distant green plains. He walked along broken, frost-cracked roads that were frequented by heavy vehicles he had to dodge constantly. The light seemed intent on leaving nothing green, revealing all in minute precision from the miniscule worm he had himself plucked out of the mud to the turning of the blue sky with his footsteps, cardboard and clear.

Choosing between the main path and a smaller track, he took the latter. It was in the shadow of a hill, and the morning dew that had soaked the ferns growing there in turn drenched his shoes and the bottom of his trousers. But it was a pleasing path that circumnavigated the slope. Halfway up, he saw the dark mouth of a cave. He looked inside as if looking for some lifeform, the movement of some animal, perhaps, the smouldering of some feline eyes. The light didn't penetrate the cave and he could only make out a deep, inhospitable gallery. Someone had written *House of Wolves* above the entrance.

He continued walking and the incline, ever steeper, made him gasp for air. The splendid view — a boundless horizon — that spread out at his feet looked back down on his route of the last two days. Below him he could make out a house that he had skirted around earlier that morning and an old, half-derelict mill. He climbed still higher, getting closer and closer to the summit.

He walked up the last few metres panting for breath. Once at the top, he was surprised by the existence of an imposing castle that he hadn't noticed from the bottom. The magnificent construction was encircled by a wall that seemed to have been cast up by the mountain itself like a stalagmite heaving itself out of the frozen earth. Inside were seven or eight buildings and towers that all rivalled each other in terms of height and beauty.

He thought back to the pomegranate that he had seen laid out dead on the ground several weeks before, its dusty stained-glass colours and red seeds. He looked up. Beyond the battlements, the main castle building boasted decorative stained-glass windows that shone down light into the castle interior in multiple joyful rays. How many decades did it take them to build a castle such as this? The Wanderer imagined a remote, ancient time before the castle existed, when the whole summit was free of human hands. A time when wolves dominated the land.

> Some thousand years before, the earth was much flatter.
> There were neither cities, nor any bridges built
> to cross rivers or valleys. The tundra and the
> savannah, the lands that touch the sea, deserts, springs,
> glaciers, were calmer, free from human contact.
>
> There were many types of beast, spread out all around,
> of large or smaller hooves, well-stocked or lighter rumps.

And, high in the sky, those birds that make cross shapes when
soaring majestically, or that make sword-like
movements when turning on high to bring down their prey.

In the sea were all the fish that inspire the myths:
immortal whales and tentacled octopuses.
The earth was flatter, still virgin, without milestones:
no circuses, no theatres, only wolves' lairs.
God's longing was yet to inspire hermitages.

One should know when to call it a day, thought the Wanderer. The path back home would be very different from the one that had brought him to the foot of the castle. Perhaps he would deviate a little on the route back. In fact, he hadn't followed any pre-established path — a road to nowhere —throughout his entire outward journey. Would he remember the route he had taken? Certainly not. But, what was it doing now?

He looked up to the sky. Some threatening clouds were growing dark to the east and that part of the sky was starting to turn a meaty blue. It was time to go back. If a storm came, he would look for shelter.

He sat at the foot of the castle for around an hour and ate berries that he had picked earlier in the day. They would have gone well with a piece of bread, but he had none.

After resting, he once again picked up his path, not knowing where he was going. His resolve, however, was unshakeable.